THE CANADIAN LIVING
COOKING
COLLECTION

EASY
MAIN DISHES

The following Canadian companies were involved in the production
of this Collection: Colour Technologies, Fred Bird & Associates Limited,
Gordon Sibley Design Inc., On-line Graphics, Telemedia Publishing Inc. and
The Madison Book Group Inc.

Canadian Living is a trademark of Telemedia Publishing Inc.
All trademark rights, registered and unregistered, are reserved.

We acknowledge the contribution of
Drew Warner, Joie Warner and Flavor Publications.

Produced by
The Madison Book Group Inc.
40 Madison Avenue
Toronto, Ontario
Canada
M5R 2S1

EASY MAIN DISHES

■ *On our cover:*
Pork Chops with
Fruit (p. 38)

Here are more than 60 ways to put the zing back into everyday cooking. Fast and tasty main-dish recipes like *Ginger-Garlic Chicken Breasts, Mini-Meat Loaves with Swiss Cheese, Crunchy Pork Chops with Parmesan, Salmon Corn Cakes with Cucumber Dill Sauce* or *Crusty Mustard Lamb Chops* are sure to become favorites for family suppers and casual weekend entertaining. You'll also find handy microwave shortcuts, serving suggestions, make-ahead tips and more!

Easy Main Dishes is just one of the eight full-color cookbooks that make up THE CANADIAN LIVING COOKING COLLECTION. Inside each of these colorful cookbooks are the kind of satisfying, easy-to-make dishes you'll want to cook over and over again. Each recipe in the Collection has been carefully selected and tested by *Canadian Living* to make sure it turns out wonderfully every time you make it. When you collect all eight cookbooks, you can choose from over 500 dishes — from marvelous soups to sensational desserts — all guaranteed to make any meal extra special.

Elizabeth Baird

Elizabeth Baird
Food Director, *Canadian Living* Magazine

Knife-and-Fork Chicken Tacos

Popular with all ages, this warm sandwich just needs to be topped with a little sour cream or yogurt.

1 lb	boneless skinless chicken breasts	500 g
4	flour tortillas (8 inches/20 cm)	4
1	onion, sliced	1
	Salt and pepper	

MARINADE

3 tbsp	vegetable oil	50 mL
3 tbsp	lime juice	50 mL
1 tbsp	Worcestershire sauce	15 mL
2	cloves garlic, minced	2
1 tsp	cumin	5 mL
Pinch	hot pepper flakes	Pinch

TOPPINGS

1/2 cup	salsa or taco sauce	125 mL
1/2 cup	shredded cheese	125 mL
1/2 cup	chopped sweet green pepper	125 mL
1 cup	shredded lettuce	250 mL

■ **Marinade:** In bowl, combine 1 tbsp (15 mL) of the oil, lime juice, Worcestershire sauce, garlic, cumin and hot pepper flakes. Slice chicken crosswise into 1/2-inch (1 cm) wide strips; toss with marinade. Let stand for 10 minutes. Drain and pat dry, reserving marinade.

■ Meanwhile, wrap tortillas in foil; warm in 350°F (180°C) oven for 10 minutes or until heated. (Alternatively, just before serving, microwave between paper towels at Medium-High/70% for 30 seconds.)

■ In skillet, heat 1 tbsp (15 mL) of the remaining oil over high heat; stir-fry chicken for 4 to 5 minutes or until no longer pink inside. Remove chicken and set aside. Add remaining oil to skillet; stir-fry onion for 1 minute. Pour in reserved marinade; cook, stirring, for 30 seconds or until most of the liquid has evaporated. Return chicken to skillet and heat through. Season with salt and pepper to taste.

■ **Toppings:** Spoon salsa onto tortillas; top with chicken mixture. Sprinkle with cheese, green pepper and lettuce. Fold tortillas in half. Makes 4 servings.

Microwave Cajun Chicken Fingers

This dish is quick; it takes only 15 minutes. Let the kids make it.

4	boneless skinless chicken breasts (about 1 lb/500 g)	4
1/3 cup	mayonnaise	75 mL
2 tsp	lemon juice	10 mL
1/2 tsp	Worcestershire sauce	2 mL
1/4 tsp	dry mustard	1 mL
1	clove garlic, minced	1
1/2 cup	fine dry bread crumbs	125 mL
1/4 cup	cornmeal	50 mL
1 tsp	paprika	5 mL
1/2 tsp	dried oregano	2 mL
1/2 tsp	black pepper	2 mL
Pinch	cayenne pepper	Pinch
	Salt	
	Dipping Sauce (recipe follows)	

■ Cut chicken on diagonal into 1/2-inch (1 cm) wide strips; set aside.

■ In small bowl, combine mayonnaise, lemon juice, Worcestershire sauce, mustard and garlic; set aside. In pie plate, combine bread crumbs, cornmeal, paprika, oregano, black and cayenne peppers, mixing well.

■ Dip chicken into mayonnaise mixture, then into crumb mixture, pressing to coat. Arrange half of the chicken fingers on microwave rack. Microwave, uncovered, at High for 2 to 3 minutes or until no longer pink inside, rotating dish once. Transfer to serving dish. Repeat with remaining chicken. Season with salt to taste. Serve with Dipping Sauce. Makes 4 servings.

DIPPING SAUCE		
1/4 cup	plain yogurt	50 mL
1/4 cup	mayonnaise	50 mL
2 tbsp	red pepper jelly	25 mL

■ In small bowl, combine yogurt, mayonnaise and jelly. Makes about 1/2 cup (125 mL).

Ginger-Garlic Chicken Breasts

This quick and easy way to prepare chicken tastes delicious. Use a mini-chopper to chop garlic and gingerroot; otherwise chop as finely as possible. Serve with wax beans and rice dotted with chopped sweet yellow pepper.

1 lb	boneless skinless chicken breasts	500 g
2 tbsp	lemon juice	25 mL
2 tsp	minced gingerroot	10 mL
2	cloves garlic, minced	2
2 tsp	olive oil	10 mL
1 tsp	cumin	5 mL
	Pepper	

■ Between waxed paper, pound chicken breasts until flattened to 1/2-inch (1 cm) thickness. Combine lemon juice, gingerroot, garlic, oil and cumin; spread over chicken. Marinate for 10 minutes at room temperature. Grill on lightly greased grill over medium-hot coals or at medium-high setting or broil for 2 to 3 minutes on each side or until no longer pink inside. Season with pepper to taste. Makes 4 servings.

Chicken and Apple Sauté

Use Cortland, Empire or Golden Delicious apples because they'll keep their shape during cooking. Serve with egg noodles and a green salad.

4 tsp	vegetable oil	20 mL
2	tart apples (unpeeled), thinly sliced	2
1	onion, sliced	1
1/2 tsp	dried thyme	2 mL
4	boneless skinless chicken breasts	4
1 cup	apple juice	250 mL
1 tbsp	cider vinegar	15 mL
1 tbsp	cornstarch	15 mL
	Salt and pepper	

■ In heavy skillet, heat 2 tsp (10 mL) of the oil over medium-high heat; cook apples, onion and thyme for about 4 minutes or just until tender-crisp. Remove to bowl and set aside.

■ Heat remaining oil in skillet; cook chicken, turning once, for 2 to 3 minutes or until golden brown. Reduce heat to medium-low. Set 1 tbsp (15 mL) apple juice aside; pour remaining apple juice into skillet along with vinegar. Cover and simmer for 6 to 8 minutes or until chicken is no longer pink inside. With slotted spoon, remove chicken to platter; keep warm.

■ Combine cornstarch with reserved apple juice; stir into skillet and cook over high heat, stirring and scraping up any browned bits on bottom of pan, for 2 minutes or until thickened. Return apple mixture to skillet and heat through; season with salt and pepper to taste. Spoon over or around chicken.

Makes 4 servings.

Chicken Burger Melts

Ground chicken, which has become available in many supermarkets across the country, is perfect for burgers. You can just as quickly broil or grill them on the barbecue.

1	egg white	1
1/2 cup	minced green onions	125 mL
1/4 cup	minced fresh parsley	50 mL
2 tbsp	dry bread crumbs	25 mL
2 tbsp	water	25 mL
1 tsp	Dijon mustard	5 mL
1/4 tsp	each salt and dried basil or thyme	1 mL
1	clove garlic, minced	1
1 lb	ground chicken	500 g
6	slices cheese	6

■ In bowl, whisk egg white; whisk in onions, parsley, bread crumbs, water, mustard, salt, basil and garlic. Mix in chicken and shape into 6 patties about 1/2 inch (1 cm) thick.

■ In lightly greased nonstick skillet over medium heat, cook patties for about 5 minutes per side or until golden brown and no longer pink inside. Top with cheese slices; cover pan and cook for 1 to 2 minutes or until cheese melts. Makes 6 servings.

Microwave Tarragon Chicken

Use your microwave oven to make this simple and satisfying dish.

4	chicken breasts, skinned and boned	4
3 tbsp	finely chopped shallots	50 mL
1/4 cup	chicken stock	50 mL
2 tbsp	tarragon vinegar	25 mL
2/3 cup	light cream	150 mL
1 tbsp	cornstarch	15 mL
1 tbsp	grainy mustard	15 mL
1-1/2 tsp	dried tarragon	7 mL
	Salt and pepper	

■ Arrange chicken around outside of 10-inch (25 cm) microwaveable pie plate; sprinkle with shallots. Combine stock and vinegar; pour over chicken. Cover and microwave at High for 4 to 6 minutes, turning chicken and rotating dish once, or until chicken is no longer pink inside and meat thermometer registers 185°F (85°C). Remove chicken and keep warm.

■ Blend together cream and cornstarch; stir into cooking liquid in pie plate. Microwave at High for 2 to 3 minutes or until thickened, stirring once. Stir in mustard, tarragon, and salt and pepper to taste. Arrange chicken on serving plates; pour sauce over chicken. Makes 4 servings.

Chicken Fajitas

If a fresh hot banana pepper is unavailable, substitute a few dashes of hot pepper sauce. Wear rubber gloves when preparing the pepper to prevent burning.

4	boneless skinless chicken breasts	4
1/4 cup	chicken stock	50 mL
2 tbsp	lime juice	25 mL
2	cloves garlic, minced	2
1 tsp	cumin	5 mL
1/2 tsp	ground coriander	2 mL
1/4 tsp	pepper	1 mL
4	flour tortillas (8 inches/20 cm)	4
2 tbsp	vegetable oil	25 mL
1	onion, thinly sliced	1
1	small sweet red pepper, cut in thin strips	1
1	hot banana pepper, cut in thin strips	1
	Salt	
	GARNISH	
	Salsa or taco sauce (optional)	
1	tomato, chopped	1
	Sour cream	

■ Slice chicken crosswise into 1/2-inch (1 cm) wide strips. In bowl, combine stock, lime juice, garlic, cumin, coriander and pepper. Add chicken and stir to coat; set aside.

■ Wrap tortillas in foil and warm in 350°F (180°C) oven for about 10 minutes or until heated through.

■ Meanwhile, in skillet, heat 1 tbsp (15 mL) of the oil over high heat. Drain chicken, reserving marinade. Pat chicken dry and add to skillet; stir-fry for 4 to 5 minutes or until no longer pink inside. Remove and set aside.

■ Add remaining oil to skillet; stir-fry onion and red and banana peppers for 1 minute. Pour in reserved marinade; cook, stirring, for 30 seconds or until most of the liquid has evaporated. Return chicken to skillet and heat through. Season with salt to taste.

■ **Garnish:** Spoon salsa (if using) and tomato over each warm tortilla; top with chicken mixture. Fold up tortillas and garnish filling with dollop of sour cream. Makes 4 servings.

Rosy Rosemary Wings

They're the easiest wings to make — and very tasty, too.

2 lb	chicken wings	1 kg
1 tbsp	lemon juice	15 mL
1-1/2 tsp	paprika	7 mL
1-1/2 tsp	crushed dried rosemary	7 mL
1-1/2 tsp	vegetable oil	7 mL
	Salt and pepper	

■ Remove tips from chicken wings and reserve for stock if desired; separate wings at joints.

■ In shallow glass dish, toss wings with lemon juice, paprika, rosemary and oil. Cover and marinate in refrigerator for 1 to 8 hours.

■ Arrange wings on broiler pan. Broil 4 inches (10 cm) from heat for 10 minutes. Turn wings over and broil for 5 to 10 minutes longer or until browned and crisp. Season with salt and pepper to taste. Makes about 30 pieces.

Chicken-Vegetable Stew

Rabbit can be used as an alternative to chicken in this vegetable-rich stew.

2 tsp	vegetable oil	10 mL
1-1/2 lb	chicken legs and thighs	750 g
1	red onion, chopped	1
3	cloves garlic, minced	3
1/4 tsp	hot pepper flakes	1 mL
3	carrots	3
3	stalks celery	3
3	large potatoes, peeled	3
1	can (19 oz/540 mL) plum tomatoes	1
1 cup	dry red wine or beef stock	250 mL
1 cup	drained chick-peas	250 mL
	Salt and pepper	
3 tbsp	chopped fresh parsley	50 mL

■ In heavy nonstick Dutch oven, heat oil over medium-high heat; brown chicken for 5 minutes on each side. Remove chicken and set aside.

■ Drain off all but 1 tsp (5 mL) fat from pot. Add onion, garlic and hot pepper flakes; cook for 5 minutes or until softened.

■ Meanwhile, cut carrots, celery and potatoes into 1-1/2-inch (4 cm) chunks; add to pot. Stir in tomatoes, breaking up with spoon. Add chicken and wine; bring to boil. Reduce heat to low; cover and simmer for 35 to 45 minutes or until chicken is tender and juices run clear when pierced. Add chick-peas and cook for 10 minutes. Season with salt and pepper to taste. Sprinkle with parsley. Makes 4 servings.

Oven-Barbecued Turkey Drumsticks

A zesty sauce adds lots of flavor and keeps inexpensive drumsticks moist through a slow roasting. Serve with mashed potatoes or rice and green peas.

2 tbsp	vegetable oil	25 mL
1	small onion, chopped	1
2 tbsp	packed brown sugar	25 mL
3/4 cup	ketchup	175 mL
1/4 cup	lemon juice	50 mL
1 tbsp	Worcestershire sauce	15 mL
1 tbsp	Dijon mustard	15 mL
1 tsp	chili powder	5 mL
Dash	hot pepper sauce	Dash
6	small turkey drumsticks (3 lb/1.5 kg)	6

■ In small heavy saucepan, heat oil over medium heat; cook onion, stirring, for 3 minutes or until softened but not browned.

■ Reduce heat to low; stir in sugar and cook, stirring, for 2 minutes. Remove from heat; stir in ketchup, lemon juice, Worcestershire sauce, mustard, chili powder and hot pepper sauce.

■ Arrange drumsticks in single layer in 13- × 9-inch (3 L) nonaluminum baking dish; pour sauce evenly over top. Cover and bake in 350°F (180°C) oven, basting occasionally, for 1 hour. Skim off any fat from sauce. Uncover and bake for 45 minutes longer or until tender and juices run clear when turkey is pierced with knife. Makes 6 servings.

Café Chicken

Coffee is the secret ingredient in this tangy sauce. Serve with rice and your favorite green vegetable.

1/4 cup	strong coffee	50 mL
1/4 cup	ketchup	50 mL
2 tbsp	packed brown sugar	25 mL
2 tbsp	Worcestershire sauce	25 mL
1 tbsp	vinegar	15 mL
1 tbsp	lemon juice	15 mL
4	chicken legs (2 lb/1 kg total)	4

■ In small saucepan or microwaveable measure, combine coffee, ketchup, sugar, Worcestershire sauce, vinegar and lemon juice; bring to boil. Reduce heat to low and simmer for 5 minutes. (Or microwave at High for 2 to 3 minutes or until bubbling, then at Medium/50% for 2 minutes, stirring once.)

■ Arrange chicken in single layer in shallow baking dish; pour sauce over chicken. Cover and marinate in refrigerator for 1 to 8 hours. Bake in 375°F (190°C) oven for 45 to 50 minutes, basting often with sauce, or until golden brown and juices run clear when chicken is pierced with fork. Makes 4 servings.

Beef Enchiladas

Use leftover roast beef in this tasty family dish, or buy a piece of roast beef at the deli and cube it.

1 tbsp	vegetable oil	15 mL
1	onion, sliced	1
1	sweet green pepper, sliced	1
1	sweet red or yellow pepper, sliced	1
1	clove garlic, minced	1
2 cups	cubed cooked roast beef (about 3/4 lb/375 g)	500 mL
1-1/2 cups	taco sauce	375 mL
1 tsp	cumin	5 mL
	Pepper	
6	flour tortillas (7 inches/18 cm)	6
1 cup	shredded Cheddar cheese	250 mL
1/2 cup	sour cream	125 mL
2 tbsp	chopped green onion	25 mL

■ In skillet, heat oil over medium heat; cook onion, green and red peppers and garlic for about 3 minutes or until onion is softened and peppers are tender-crisp. Remove from heat; stir in roast beef, 1/2 cup (125 mL) of the taco sauce, cumin, and pepper to taste.

■ Spoon about 3/4 cup (175 mL) of the meat mixture down centre of each tortilla. Sprinkle with 1 tbsp (15 mL) of the cheese. Fold tortilla over filling, overlapping edges slightly. Arrange, seam side up, in 11- × 7-inch (2 L) baking or microwaveable dish. Spoon remaining taco sauce over tortillas; spoon sour cream down centre.

■ **Conventional method:** Sprinkle with remaining cheese. Bake in 350°F (180°C) oven for about 30 minutes or until heated through. Sprinkle with green onion.

■ **Microwave method:** Cover with vented plastic wrap; microwave at Medium (50%) for 8 to 10 minutes or until heated through, rotating twice. Sprinkle with remaining cheese and green onion. Cover and let stand for 3 minutes.

■ Makes 6 servings.

Saucy Beef Stew

Brown the meat while the rest of the stew comes to a boil, then let them simmer together in a slow oven. If desired, stir in extra cooked vegetables (potato cubes, turnip slices, parsnip pieces) before serving with lots of crusty bread to capture the sauce.

2 lb	stewing beef, cubed	1 kg
1/4 cup	all-purpose flour	50 mL
1/2 tsp	salt	2 mL
1/4 tsp	pepper	1 mL
2 cups	beef stock	500 mL
1/2 cup	dry red wine	125 mL
1	can (14 oz/398 mL) tomatoes (undrained)	1
5	carrots, sliced	5
2	onions, sliced	2
1-1/2 cups	sliced mushrooms (1/4 lb/125 g)	375 mL
1/2 tsp	crushed dried rosemary	2 mL

■ In bag, toss beef with flour, salt and pepper. Arrange beef on baking sheet; bake in 500°F (260°C) oven for 10 to 15 minutes or until lightly browned.

■ Meanwhile, in large Dutch oven, combine beef stock, wine, tomatoes, carrots, onions, mushrooms and rosemary, breaking up tomatoes with fork; bring to boil. Add browned beef; bake in 300°F (150°C) oven for 2 hours or until beef is tender. Makes about 6 servings.

Mini-Meat Loaves with Swiss Cheese

Traditional meat loaf gets a lift from a Swiss cheese filling. These individual servings mean less cooking time, so dinner can be on the table in a half-hour.

1 lb	ground beef	500 g
1/4 cup	dry bread crumbs	50 mL
1	egg, lightly beaten	1
2 tbsp	finely chopped onion	25 mL
1/2 tsp	salt	2 mL
1/4 tsp	pepper	1 mL
1 cup	shredded Swiss cheese	250 mL
1/4 cup	diced sweet green pepper	50 mL
2 tbsp	mayonnaise	25 mL
1 tsp	Dijon mustard	5 mL
1 tsp	Worcestershire sauce	5 mL

■ In bowl, combine ground beef, bread crumbs, egg, onion, salt and pepper. In small bowl, mix together Swiss cheese, green pepper, mayonnaise, mustard and Worcestershire sauce.

■ Divide beef mixture into 8 oval patties. Top 4 ovals with cheese mixture; cover with remaining ovals, pressing edges firmly together.

■ Place meat loaves on rack in 13- × 9-inch (3.5 L) baking dish. Bake in 375°F (190°C) oven for 25 to 30 minutes or until browned and no longer pink inside. Makes 4 servings.

Saucy Beef Stew ▶

Meat Loaf with Gravy

This is a good old-fashioned meat loaf, moist and tender with lots of flavor. Serve with mashed potatoes to soak up the gravy.

1/2 lb	ground beef	250 g
1/2 lb	lean ground pork	250 g
1/2 lb	ground veal	250 g
1	onion, finely chopped	1
1	large stalk celery, finely chopped	1
1	large carrot, grated	1
3/4 cup	rolled oats	175 mL
1/2 cup	skim milk powder	125 mL
2 cups	beef stock	500 mL
1 tsp	dried thyme	5 mL
1/2 tsp	each dried sage, salt, pepper and mustard	2 mL
Pinch	allspice	Pinch
2 tbsp	all-purpose flour	25 mL
	Gravy browning (optional)	

■ In bowl, combine beef, pork, veal, onion, celery, carrot, oats and skim milk powder; mix well. Add 1/2 cup (125 mL) of the beef stock, thyme, sage, salt, pepper, mustard and allspice; combine thoroughly. Transfer to 8- × 4-inch (1.5 L) loaf pan.

■ Bake in 350°F (180°C) oven for 30 minutes; pour 1/2 cup (125 mL) of the remaining stock over and cook for 45 minutes longer or until meat is well browned and meat thermometer registers 170°F (75°C).

■ Blend flour with remaining 1 cup (250 mL) stock. Drain pan juices into saucepan; stir in stock mixture and cook, stirring, over medium-high heat until thickened. Add a few drops of gravy browning (if using). Serve with meat loaf. Makes about 6 servings.

(left to right) Meat Loaf with Chili Sauce (p. 20); Cheese Meat Loaf Pinwheel with Spinach Mushroom Filling; Meat Loaf with Gravy ▶

Cheese Meat Loaf Pinwheel with Spinach Mushroom Filling

Served either hot or cold, round slices of this meat loaf make an attractive pinwheel pattern on the plate.

1 lb	ground beef	500 g	1 cup	sliced mushrooms	250 mL
1/2 lb	lean ground pork	250 g	1/2 cup	chopped onion	125 mL
1 cup	shredded Cheddar cheese	250 mL	1/4 cup	chopped fresh parsley	50 mL
1/2 cup	fine dry bread crumbs	125 mL	1/2 cup	fine dry bread crumbs	125 mL
1	egg, beaten	1	1	egg	1
2 tsp	Worcestershire sauce	10 mL	1/2 tsp	salt	2 mL
3/4 tsp	salt	4 mL	Pinch	each pepper and nutmeg	Pinch
1/4 tsp	pepper	1 mL			

	FILLING	
1	pkg (10 oz/300 g) spinach, trimmed	1
1/4 cup	butter	50 mL

■ **Filling:** Rinse spinach; shake off excess water. With just the water clinging to leaves, cook spinach until wilted; drain and squeeze out excess moisture. Chop coarsely and set aside.

■ In skillet, melt butter over medium heat; cook mushrooms and onion until onion is transluscent. Transfer to bowl. Add spinach, parsley, bread crumbs, egg, salt, pepper and nutmeg; mix well.

■ In bowl, combine beef, pork, cheese, bread crumbs, egg, Worcestershire sauce, salt and pepper. Place meat mixture between two sheets of waxed paper; roll into 18- × 8-inch (45 × 20 cm) rectangle. Remove top sheet. Spread spinach mixture evenly over meat, leaving 1/2-inch (1 cm) border. Roll up meat from short end in jelly-roll style, lifting with paper. Ease loaf into 8- × 4-inch (1.5 L) loaf pan. Bake in 350°F (180°C) oven for about 1 hour or until browned and meat thermometer registers 170°F (75°C). Makes about 6 servings.

Meat Loaf with Chili Sauce

This is the simplest of meat loaves to make. Chili sauce adds flavor and color.

1-1/2 lb	ground beef	750 g
3/4 cup	rolled oats	175 mL
1	carrot, grated	1
1/2 cup	finely chopped onion	125 mL
1/2 cup	milk	125 mL
1	egg, beaten	1
2 tsp	Worcestershire sauce	10 mL
1/2 tsp	each dry mustard and salt	2 mL
1/4 tsp	pepper	1 mL
1/2 cup	chili sauce	125 mL

■ In bowl, combine beef, oats, carrot, onion, milk, egg, Worcestershire sauce, mustard, salt and pepper; mix thoroughly. Transfer to 8- × 4-inch (1.5 L) loaf pan. Spoon half of the chili sauce over meat. Bake in 350°F (180°C) oven for about 1 hour or until meat is browned and meat thermometer registers 170°F (75°C). Serve with remaining chili sauce. Makes about 6 servings.

Barbecued Orange Soy Steak

Everyone will enjoy succulent beef flavored with a hint of orange.

2 lb	boneless blade or chuck short rib steak (1 inch/2.5 cm thick), trimmed	1 kg
	MARINADE	
1/2 cup	soy sauce	125 mL
1/4 cup	vinegar	50 mL
1/4 cup	orange juice	50 mL
2 tbsp	orange marmalade	25 mL
1	clove garlic, crushed	1
1 tsp	minced hot green chili pepper (or 1/4 tsp/1 mL crushed dried chilies)	5 mL

■ **Marinade:** In nonmetallic shallow dish, combine soy sauce, vinegar, orange juice, marmalade, garlic and chili; mix well. Add beef and turn to coat. Cover and refrigerate for at least 8 or up to 24 hours, turning occasionally.
■ Remove steak from marinade, reserving marinade. Place on greased grill over medium-hot coals or at medium setting; cook, brushing occasionally with marinade, for 4 to 5 minutes per side or until medium-rare. To serve, cut diagonally into thin slices. Makes about 6 servings.

Quick Chili con Carne

Here's a delicious, mild chili recipe that yields plenty for dinner, with leftovers, too. Top with shredded cheese, shredded lettuce or sour cream if desired. If you prefer a little more spice, add more chili powder.

1 tbsp	vegetable oil	15 mL
2 lb	lean ground beef	1 kg
1 cup	coarsely chopped onions	250 mL
1	large sweet green pepper, cut in 1/2-inch (1 cm) pieces	1
2	cloves garlic, minced	2
2 tbsp	chili powder	25 mL
2 tsp	dried oregano	10 mL
2 tsp	cumin	10 mL
1-1/2 tsp	salt	7 mL
	Pepper	
1	can (28 oz/796 mL) tomatoes (undrained)	1
2	cans (each 19 oz/540 mL) kidney beans, drained	2

■ In Dutch oven or large saucepan, heat oil over medium-high heat; cook beef, stirring to break up, onions, green pepper and garlic until beef is browned and vegetables are tender, 6 to 8 minutes.

■ Stir in chili powder, oregano, cumin, salt, and pepper to taste; add tomatoes and bring to boil. Reduce heat and simmer, uncovered, for 20 minutes or until thickened slightly, stirring occasionally.

■ Add kidney beans and heat through, stirring often. Serve in soup bowls. Makes 6 to 8 servings.

CHILI IN A JIFFY
There are as many variations of chili as there are cooks. But few are as fast and easy as our Quick Chili con Carne. Just combine the ingredients and let simmer while you pop a batch of Cornmeal Muffins (see Muffins and Cookies, p. 11) into the oven. When the muffins are ready, so is dinner. For dessert, chop up a few apples (or pears, bananas or mangoes), mix with plain yogurt and sprinkle lightly with cinnamon.

Beef and Pepper Stir-Fry

Oyster sauce is available in Oriental food stores. Assemble all the ingredients before you begin stir-frying. Serve with rice.

1/2 lb	beef tenderloin or sirloin steak	250 g
1 tbsp	red wine vinegar	15 mL
1 tbsp	soy sauce	15 mL
2 tsp	minced gingerroot	10 mL
1	large clove garlic, minced	1
2 tbsp	vegetable oil	25 mL
1	onion, thinly sliced	1
1	each sweet green and red pepper, cut in strips	1
2 tbsp	oyster sauce	25 mL
1/2 tsp	sesame oil	2 mL
1 tsp	cornstarch	5 mL
1/4 cup	beef stock	50 mL

■ Cut beef across the grain into thin slices about 2 inches (5 cm) long and 1/8 inch (3 mm) thick. In small bowl, combine beef, vinegar, soy sauce, gingerroot and garlic; cover and marinate at room temperature for 30 minutes.

■ In wok or large skillet, heat 1 tbsp (15 mL) of the oil over high heat; stir-fry beef mixture for about 2 minutes or until browned. Remove beef and juices from wok; reserve.

■ Heat remaining oil in wok; stir-fry onion and green and red peppers for about 2 minutes or until tender-crisp. Return beef and juices to wok. Stir in oyster sauce and sesame oil.

■ Dissolve cornstarch in 1 tbsp (15 mL) of the stock. Stir remaining stock and cornstarch mixture into pan; cook for about 1 minute or until slightly thickened, stirring constantly. Makes 2 servings.

Microwave Beef Carbonade

This microwave version of a long-simmering stew takes only 40 minutes. Because the meat and onions are browned on top of the stove, none of the rich taste or color is missing.

1 lb	stewing beef, cut in 1-inch (2.5 cm) cubes	500 g
2 tbsp	all-purpose flour	25 mL
1 tbsp	vegetable oil	15 mL
4 cups	sliced onions	1 L
1	clove garlic, minced	1
1/3 cup	water	75 mL
3/4 cup	beef stock	175 mL
1/2 cup	beer or beef stock	125 mL
1 tsp	dried thyme	5 mL
1	bay leaf	1
Pinch	each allspice, salt and pepper	Pinch
1	carrot, chopped	1
1	stalk celery, chopped	1
1 tsp	red wine vinegar	5 mL

■ Toss beef cubes with flour. In large skillet, heat oil over medium-high heat; add meat and cook for 6 to 8 minutes or until browned all over. Transfer to 12-cup (3 L) microwaveable casserole; set aside.

■ Add onions and garlic to skillet; stir up brown bits and pour in water. Cook for 8 to 10 minutes or until deep golden brown; add to meat. Add beef stock, beer, thyme, bay leaf, allspice, salt and pepper. Cover and microwave at High for 5 minutes or until boiling; stir. Cover and microwave at Medium (50%) for 20 minutes.

■ Stir in carrot and celery; cover and microwave at Medium (50%) for 25 to 30 minutes or until meat is tender. Remove bay leaf. Stir in vinegar; let stand for 5 minutes. Makes 4 servings.

Grilled Caribbean Beef Kabobs

Nicely glazed and with a hint of spicy heat, these kabobs are a perfect way to enjoy a taste of the tropics in your own backyard.

2 lb	boneless blade or chuck short rib steak (1-inch/2.5 cm thick)	1 kg
	MARINADE	
1/2 cup	lemon or lime juice	125 mL
1/4 cup	vegetable oil	50 mL
3 tbsp	liquid honey	50 mL
1 tbsp	minced hot pepper	15 mL
1 tbsp	minced gingerroot	15 mL
1 tbsp	soy sauce	15 mL
1-1/2 tsp	allspice	7 mL
1/2 tsp	cinnamon	2 mL
1/4 tsp	cloves	1 mL

■ Trim steak; cut meat into 1-inch (2.5 cm) cubes.

■ **Marinade:** In nonmetallic bowl, whisk together lemon juice, oil, honey, hot pepper, gingerroot, soy sauce, allspice, cinnamon and cloves; add beef cubes, stirring to coat. Cover and refrigerate for at least 8 or up to 24 hours, stirring occasionally.

■ Reserving marinade, thread meat onto greased metal skewers. Place on greased grill over medium-hot coals or at medium setting; cook, turning once and basting occasionally with marinade, for 7 to 10 minutes or until browned outside and pink inside. Makes 6 servings.

Saturday Simmer

Nothing could be simpler to prepare yet as full-flavored and satisfying as this effortless one-pot meal. It's perfect with crusty garlic bread. As a bonus, you'll have plenty of beef stock left over to use for soup the next day.

2	cans (each 10 oz/284 mL) undiluted beef broth	2
3-1/2 lb	beef short ribs	1.75 kg
4	onions	4
8	small carrots	8
4	parsnips	4
1/4 cup	chopped fresh parsley	50 mL

■ In large pot, pour broth over ribs. Add enough water to cover (about 6 cups/1.5 L). Bring to boil and skim off foam; reduce heat to medium-low and simmer, partially covered, for 2 hours or until meat is tender.

■ Cut onions in half lengthwise without trimming ends. Add to pot along with carrots and parsnips; partially cover and cook for 20 to 25 minutes or until vegetables are tender.

■ Remove meat and vegetables; arrange on platter. Skim fat from broth. Spoon a little broth over meat and vegetables; sprinkle with parsley. Pass remaining broth separately. Makes 4 servings.

Skillet Eggplant Beef

This skillet supper has wonderful Middle Eastern flavors. Serve with warm pita bread and a lettuce salad with orange slices and black olives.

1	eggplant (about 1 lb/500 g)	1
	Salt	
1 lb	ground beef	500 g
1	small onion, chopped	1
1	clove garlic, minced	1
1/2 cup	dry red wine or water	125 mL
1	can (7-1/2 oz/213 mL) tomato sauce	1
2 tbsp	chopped fresh parsley	25 mL
3/4 tsp	dried oregano	4 mL
1/2 tsp	cinnamon	2 mL
1/4 tsp	pepper	1 mL
1 cup	shredded mozzarella cheese (about 4 oz/125 g)	250 mL
	Paprika	
	Freshly grated Parmesan cheese	

■ Peel eggplant and cut into 1/2-inch (1 cm) thick slices; sprinkle lightly with salt and spread out in single layer on paper towels.

■ Meanwhile, in large skillet, cook beef, onion and garlic over medium-high heat, breaking up meat with wooden spoon, for about 5 minutes or until browned. Drain off excess fat. Stir in wine, tomato sauce, parsley, oregano, cinnamon and pepper.

■ Pat eggplant dry; overlap slices on top of meat mixture. Reduce heat to low; cover and simmer for about 20 minutes or until eggplant is tender, turning slices once.

■ Top with mozzarella and sprinkle with paprika to taste. Serve immediately. Pass Parmesan cheese separately. Makes about 4 servings.

LIGHT AND HEALTHY BEEF
Ground beef is inexpensive and very nutritious. All cuts of beef, even ground, are excellent sources of iron, complete protein, zinc and niacin. Look for lean ground beef that contains no more than 17 per cent fat and remember to drain off any excess fat after browning the meat.

Feta Cheese Burgers

Serve these juicy burgers, inspired by Middle Eastern flavors, in warm pita breads.

1-1/2 lb	lean ground beef	750 g
1/2 tsp	salt	2 mL
1/4 tsp	pepper	1 mL
1/4 tsp	cumin	1 mL
2 oz	feta cheese	50 g
2 tbsp	chopped fresh mint (or 2 tsp/10 mL dried)	25 mL

■ In bowl, combine beef, salt, pepper and cumin; divide into 4 portions. Cut cheese into 4 cubes; flatten cubes and sprinkle with mint. Form 4 meat patties with cheese and mint buried in centre of each patty.

■ On greased grill or in skillet, cook patties over hot coals or at medium-high setting for 12 to 14 minutes, turning once, or until no longer pink inside. Makes 4 servings.

Teriyaki Roast Beef

Light Japanese soy sauce is best for keeping the salt-sweet flavor of this distinctive roast subtle. A fine hot dish, it's also good served at room temperature.

1/2 cup	light soy sauce	125 mL
1/2 cup	sweet Japanese rice wine or semi-dry sherry	125 mL
2	cloves garlic, minced	2
4 tsp	granulated sugar	20 mL
1 tbsp	grated gingerroot	15 mL
1	outside round boneless roast of beef, about 4 lb (2 kg)	1
2 tsp	sesame seeds	10 mL
1/2 cup	water	125 mL
1/4 cup	beef stock	50 mL
1 tbsp	cornstarch	15 mL
1 tbsp	minced green onion	15 mL

■ In deep bowl large enough to hold roast, combine soy sauce, rice wine, garlic, sugar and gingerroot. Add beef and turn several times to coat, leaving fat side up. Cover and refrigerate, turning periodically, for 8 hours or up to 24 hours.

■ Place beef on rack in roasting pan, reserving marinade. Set 1/4 cup (50 mL) marinade aside for sauce. Roast, uncovered, in 375°F (190°C) oven for 15 minutes. Reduce heat to 325°F (160°C); roast, basting every 15 minutes with remaining marinade and pan juices, for about 2 hours longer or until meat thermometer registers 140°F (60°C) for medium-rare or until desired doneness. Transfer to warm platter; tent with foil and let stand for 15 minutes.

■ Meanwhile, in small skillet, toast sesame seeds over low heat until golden and fragrant, shaking pan occasionally. In food processor or mini-chopper, process seeds until texture of coarse sand; set aside.

■ In saucepan over medium heat, combine reserved marinade, water and stock. Dissolve cornstarch in 1 tbsp (15 mL) water; stir into sauce. Bring to boil and cook, stirring, for 1 minute or until thickened. Stir in sesame seeds and green onion.

■ To serve, slice beef thinly and arrange on platter; spoon sauce over. Makes 6 to 8 servings.

Ground Beef and Mushroom Pizza on Biscuit Crust

Easy to make, this satisfying dish is perfect for a family of pizza lovers. For a light dessert, serve refreshing sherbet.

2 tbsp	butter	25 mL
1 lb	ground beef	500 g
1/2 lb	mushrooms, sliced	250 g
1	clove garlic, minced	1
1 tsp	dried oregano	5 mL
Pinch	hot pepper flakes	Pinch
	Salt and pepper	
1	can (7-1/2 oz/213 mL) tomato sauce	1
1/2 lb	mozzarella cheese, thinly sliced	250 g
	BISCUIT BASE	
2 cups	all-purpose flour	500 mL
4 tsp	baking powder	20 mL
1 tbsp	granulated sugar	15 mL
1/2 tsp	salt	2 mL
1/2 cup	shortening	125 mL
2/3 cup	milk	150 mL
1	egg, beaten	1

■ In large skillet, melt butter over medium-high heat; cook beef, mushrooms, garlic, oregano, hot pepper flakes, and salt and pepper to taste, breaking up meat with wooden spoon, for about 5 minutes or until meat is browned. Stir in tomato sauce; cook for about 3 minutes or until thickened.

■ **Biscuit Base:** In large bowl, stir together flour, baking powder, sugar and salt. With two knives or pastry blender, cut in shortening until mixture resembles coarse crumbs. Stir together milk and egg; add all at once to flour mixture. Stir gently just until combined.

■ Turn out onto well-floured surface; with floured hands, knead gently 20 times. Press evenly into greased 12-inch (30 cm) round pizza pan. Sprinkle evenly with meat mixture; top with mozzarella. Bake in 450°F (230°C) oven for about 25 minutes or until crust is golden brown. Makes 4 generous servings.

Broiled Flank Steak with Potatoes

These potatoes are so tasty, they can easily become addictive. Round out this quick meal with frozen peas.

1-1/4 lb	flank steak	625 g
1/4 cup	minced onion	50 mL
2 tbsp	barbecue sauce	25 mL
1	clove garlic, minced	1
1/4 tsp	ginger	1 mL
	Pepper	
3	potatoes (unpeeled)	3
1/4 cup	vegetable oil	50 mL
1 tsp	dried oregano	5 mL
	Salt	

■ Score flank steak on each side in diagonal pattern; place on greased broiler pan. In small bowl, combine onion, barbecue sauce, garlic, ginger and 1/4 tsp (1 mL) pepper; brush half of the mixture over top of steak.

■ Cut potatoes into 1/2-inch (1 cm) thick slices; arrange around steak. Brush half of the oil over potatoes; sprinkle with half of the oregano and salt and pepper to taste. Broil 4 inches (10 cm) from heat for 5 minutes. Turn steak over and brush with remaining barbecue sauce mixture; broil for 4 to 6 minutes or until desired doneness. Remove steak to cutting board; tent with foil to keep warm.

■ Turn potatoes over; brush with remaining oil and sprinkle with remaining oregano. Broil for 3 to 5 minutes or until crisp. Cut steak diagonally across the grain into thin slices; season with salt and pepper to taste. Serve with potatoes. Makes 4 servings.

BROILING
Broiling is a fast and simple way of using high heat to cook tender lean cuts of meat. Remember that some fat marbling adds to the meat's flavor and tenderness. Fat will melt and drip off as the meat cooks. Slash any exterior fat before broiling to prevent curling.

• *Test for doneness by touch as well as timing. Use the flat of a fork or your finger to avoid piercing the meat and letting juices escape. For well done, meat is firm; for medium, it springs back; for rare, meat is soft. Broil meat on a rack or in a pan 4 to 6 inches (10 to 15 cm) below the heat; season with salt afterward to minimize drying out.*

• *Thin cuts of meat have to be watched carefully when broiling to avoid overcooking and drying out. Do not buy wedge-cut steaks and chops that are thick on one side and thin on the other. These will cook unevenly under the broiler.*

Cajun Burgers with Bayou Sauce

These medium-hot burgers with a zingy sauce will be a hit with everyone. Burgers hold together much better if made ahead and refrigerated.

1 lb	lean ground beef	500 g
Half	sweet green pepper, minced	Half
2	cloves garlic, minced	2
1 tsp	each cumin and dried oregano	5 mL
1/2 tsp	each dried thyme, grated lemon rind and hot pepper sauce	2 mL
1/4 tsp	salt	1 mL
4	kaiser buns, split	4
	Leaf lettuce	
	BAYOU SAUCE	
1/2 cup	mayonnaise	125 mL
1 tbsp	chili sauce	15 mL
1/2 tsp	hot pepper sauce	2 mL

■ **Bayou Sauce:** In small bowl, stir together mayonnaise, chili sauce and hot pepper sauce. Cover and refrigerate until serving time or up to 3 days.

■ In bowl, mix together beef, green pepper, garlic, cumin, oregano, thyme, lemon rind, hot pepper sauce and salt; shape into 4 patties. Cover and refrigerate for at least 1 hour or up to 8 hours.

■ Place patties on greased grill over medium-hot coals or on medium-high setting; grill for about 5 minutes per side or until well done and no longer pink inside.

■ Meanwhile, toast buns on grill. Spread bottom halves with sauce.

■ Top with patty, lettuce and remaining bun. Makes 4 servings.

Beef Creole with Rice

For more heat, add a dash of hot pepper sauce to this colorful dish.

2 cups	water or beef stock	500 mL
1 cup	long-grain rice	250 mL
1 lb	lean ground beef	500 g
1/2 cup	chopped sweet green pepper	125 mL
1/2 cup	chopped celery	125 mL
1/4 cup	chopped green onions (white and green parts)	50 mL
3	cloves garlic, minced	3
1	can (19 oz/540 mL) tomatoes (undrained)	1
1 tsp	each dried oregano and thyme	5 mL
1/2 tsp	black pepper	2 mL
1/2 tsp	cumin	2 mL
Pinch	each cayenne pepper and salt	Pinch

■ In saucepan with tight-fitting lid, bring water to boil; add rice. Cover and reduce heat to simmer; cook for 15 minutes without removing lid. Remove from heat and let stand, covered, for 3 to 5 minutes or until rice is tender.

■ Meanwhile, in large nonstick skillet over medium heat, cook beef, stirring to break up, for 5 minutes; drain off fat. Stir in green pepper, celery, onions and garlic; cook, stirring, for 5 minutes.

■ Add tomatoes, oregano, thyme, black pepper, cumin, cayenne and salt; bring to boil, breaking up tomatoes with back of spoon. Cook over medium-low heat for 10 minutes; increase heat to high and boil for about 3 minutes or until excess liquid has evaporated. Serve over rice. Makes 4 servings.

Crusty Mustard Lamb Chops

Stack a steamer with sliced carrots, brussels sprouts, diced potatoes and shredded cabbage to cook just as fast as these tasty chops.

1/3 cup	dry bread crumbs	75 mL
1	large clove garlic, minced	1
1/2 tsp	dried thyme	2 mL
1/4 tsp	pepper	1 mL
1/4 cup	Dijon mustard	50 mL
4	shoulder lamp chops (about 3/4 inch/2 cm thick)	4

■ In bowl, combine crumbs, garlic, thyme and pepper; stir in 3 tbsp (50 mL) of the mustard until combined. Trim excess fat from chops; slash edges. Brush chops all over with remaining mustard. Broil 4 inches (10 cm) from heat for 5 minutes or until browned. Turn chops over; spread crumb mixture on top. Broil for 2 to 3 minutes or until desired doneness and topping is golden. Makes 4 servings.

Cabbage Rolls

There are countless versions of cabbage rolls in kitchens across the country. This is one of the simplest and best. They're good served right out of the oven or reheated.

1	cabbage	1
1 cup	long-grain rice	250 mL
3/4 lb	salt pork, finely chopped	375 g
2	onions, finely chopped	2
	Salt	
1	can (19 oz/540 mL) tomato juice	1

■ With large sharp knife, cut out core of cabbage. Place cabbage in deep pot and pour boiling water into core until cabbage is completely covered. Let stand until outer leaves can be separated, then parboil or steam leaves just until soft and pliable. Continue with remainder of cabbage.

■ In saucepan, bring 2 cups (500 mL) water to boil; add rice. Reduce heat to low and cook, covered, for 15 minutes; drain.

■ Meanwhile, in separate saucepan, cook salt pork over medium heat until fat is melted. Add onions; cook until lightly browned. Add to cooked rice; season with salt to taste.

■ Line roasting pan with outer cabbage leaves. Place spoonful of rice mixture onto each inner cabbage leaf; roll up, tucking in ends, and place in pan. (If necessary, trim out centre rib of leaf to make rolling easier.) Pour tomato juice over rolls. Cover with more cabbage leaves. Cover and bake in 350°F (180°C) oven for 1-1/2 to 2 hours or until tender. Makes 6 to 8 servings.

Crunchy Pork Chops with Parmesan

Guests and family alike will love this casserole dish of pork chops and sautéed onions under a cheesy crust. Bake the gratin in a large open roasting pan and serve with baked potatoes, steamed brussels sprouts and a grated carrot salad.

1/4 cup	butter	50 mL
3 cups	thinly sliced onions	750 mL
1/3 cup	slivered pimiento or sweet red pepper	75 mL
1/2 tsp	salt	2 mL
1/4 tsp	pepper	1 mL
1/4 tsp	dried thyme	1 mL
6	pork loin chops (2 lb/1 kg total)	6
1 cup	chicken stock	250 mL
	GRATIN	
3/4 cup	bread crumbs	175 mL
1/2 cup	shredded Fontina or mozzarella cheese	125 mL
1/2 cup	freshly grated Parmesan cheese	125 mL
2 tbsp	butter, melted	25 mL
	GARNISH (optional)	
	Red pepper strips	
	Fresh thyme	

■ In large skillet, melt 2 tbsp (25 mL) of the butter over medium-low heat; cook onions, stirring frequently, until tender and fragrant but not browned, about 15 minutes. Stir in pimiento, salt, pepper and thyme. With slotted spoon, transfer mixture to bowl and set aside.

■ In same skillet, melt remaining butter. Brown chops, in batches if necessary, over medium-high heat, until golden on both sides.

■ In 8-cup (2 L) gratin dish, spread half of the onion mixture. Top with pork chops in overlapping rows; cover with remaining onion mixture. Drizzle stock over casserole. Cover and bake in 400°F (200°C) oven, basting 2 or 3 times, for 40 minutes or until chops are tender.

■ **Gratin:** Combine bread crumbs, Fontina and Parmesan cheeses and butter; sprinkle over casserole. Bake for 10 minutes longer to form crisp topping. Broil for about 2 minutes to brown topping if desired. Garnish with red pepper strips and thyme (if using). Makes 6 servings.

Microwave Mustard-Glazed Peameal Bacon

Lean peameal bacon with its characteristic cornmeal topping is the Cadillac of the bacon world. Here's a quick way to turn an unsliced piece into supper.

1/4 cup	apple cider	50 mL
1 lb	peameal bacon	500 g
4 tsp	packed brown sugar	20 mL
4 tsp	Dijon mustard	20 mL
Pinch	ginger	Pinch

■ In 9-inch (23 cm) microwaveable pie plate, pour apple cider over bacon; cover and microwave at Medium (50%) for 9 minutes, turning bacon over and rotating dish halfway through.

■ Combine sugar, mustard and ginger; brush over bacon. Microwave, uncovered, at Medium (50%) for 4 to 6 minutes or until bacon is heated through and glazed. Cover and let stand for 5 minutes before slicing to serve. Makes 4 servings.

Broiled Ham with Pineapple Salsa

Steamed broccoli and thinly sliced sweet potatoes round out this updated, light main course.

1	can (14 oz/398 mL) unsweetened crushed pineapple	1
1 tbsp	Dijon mustard	15 mL
4	ham steaks (about 6 oz/175 g each)	4
2 tbsp	chopped red onion	25 mL
2 tbsp	chopped fresh parsley	25 mL
1 tbsp	bottled hot salsa	15 mL
1 tbsp	lemon juice	15 mL

■ Drain pineapple, reserving 2 tbsp (25 mL) juice in small bowl; stir in mustard. Brush over ham on broiler pan; broil, without turning, for 5 to 8 minutes or until heated through and lightly browned around edges. In serving dish, combine pineapple, onion, parsley, salsa and lemon juice. Serve with ham. Makes 4 servings.

Microwave Mustard-Glazed Peameal Bacon ▶

Pork Chops with Fruit

This fresh and light sauce is fast and easy, but special enough for guests. For added color, you can add sections of a blood orange as we did for our cover photograph.

3 tbsp	butter	50 mL	2	kiwifruit, peeled and sliced in 6 sections each	2
4	pork chops (about 1-1/2 lb/750 g)	4			
2 tbsp	minced onion	25 mL			
1 tbsp	packed brown sugar	15 mL			
1 tbsp	cornstarch	15 mL			
1/2 cup	orange juice	125 mL			
1/2 cup	chicken stock	125 mL			
1/4 cup	orange liqueur (optional)	50 mL			
1 tsp	grated orange rind	5 mL			
	Salt and pepper				
1	orange, peeled and sliced	1			
1	peach, peeled, pitted and sliced	1			

■ In skillet, melt 2 tbsp (25 mL) of the butter over medium-high heat; brown chops on both sides, 8 to 10 minutes. Remove and set aside.

■ Melt remaining butter in skillet; cook onion until softened. Sprinkle with sugar.

■ Mix cornstarch with orange juice; stir into skillet along with stock, liqueur (if using) and orange rind. Bring to boil, stirring to scrape up browned bits from bottom of pan. Season with salt and pepper to taste.

■ Return chops to skillet and reduce heat; cover and simmer for about 10 minutes or until chops are tender. Top with orange, peach and kiwifruit; simmer for 1 to 2 minutes or until heated through, basting occasionally. Makes 4 servings.

Microwave Italian Sausage Sandwich with Peperonata

Sweet peppers, and lots of them, are the "peperonata" in this easy sandwich supper.

4	hot Italian sausages (about 1 lb/500 g total)	4
4	crusty Italian rolls	4
	PEPERONATA	
2 tbsp	olive oil	25 mL
1	onion, thinly sliced	1
2	cloves garlic, minced	2
1	large sweet red or yellow pepper, thinly sliced	1
1	large sweet green pepper, thinly sliced	1
2	tomatoes, seeded and chopped	2
2 tsp	each dried basil and oregano	10 mL
	Salt and pepper	

■ **Peperonata:** In 8-cup (2 L) microwaveable casserole, combine oil, onion and garlic; cover and microwave at High for 2 minutes or until onion is softened, stirring once.

■ Add red and green peppers, tomatoes, basil, oregano, and salt and pepper to taste. Cover

and microwave at High for 8 to 10 minutes or until vegetables are very tender, stirring twice. Set aside.

■ Place sausages in circle around outside of microwave roasting rack; prick. Cover with waxed paper and microwave at High for 4 to 6 minutes or until cooked through, turning sausages over and rotating dish once. Let stand for 3 minutes.

■ Meanwhile, wrap rolls loosely in paper towel; microwave at Medium-Low (30%) for 30 to 60 seconds or until warm. Slice rolls in half horizontally; sandwich sausage and one-quarter of the peperonata in each. Makes 4 servings.

Orange Pork Stir-Fry

Caramelizing sugar until golden gives this stir-fry sauce its rich color and slightly sweet flavor. Serve this colorful dish over couscous or rice.

3/4 lb	lean boneless pork	375 g
2	zucchini	2
1	sweet red or green pepper	1
2 tbsp	granulated sugar	25 mL
1/3 cup	orange juice	75 mL
2 tbsp	red wine vinegar	25 mL
2 tsp	grated orange rind	10 mL
1/4 cup	chicken stock	50 mL
1 tsp	cumin	5 mL
2 tsp	cornstarch	10 mL
2 tbsp	vegetable oil	25 mL
1-1/2 tsp	grated gingerroot	7 mL
	Salt and pepper	

■ Cut pork diagonally into 1/8-inch (3 mm) thick slices; pat dry. Cut zucchini into slices. Seed, core and cut red pepper into thin strips. Set aside.

■ In skillet or wok, heat sugar over medium heat, stirring constantly, for 2 to 3 minutes or until caramelized and golden brown. Stir in orange juice, vinegar and orange rind until sauce is smooth. Pour into 2-cup (500 mL) measure; add stock and cumin. Blend in cornstarch.

■ Wipe out skillet; heat oil over high heat. Sauté pork, stirring often, for 2 minutes or until browned; transfer to plate. Add zucchini, red pepper and gingerroot to skillet; sauté, stirring constantly, for 2 minutes. Return pork to skillet; stir in stock mixture. Cover and cook, stirring occasionally, for 2 minutes or until sauce thickens and vegetables are tender-crisp. Season with salt and pepper to taste. Makes 4 servings.

Quick and Easy Jambalaya

If it's available, use Black Forest ham instead of regular cooked ham for extra flavor.

8	slices bacon, chopped	8
2 tbsp	butter	25 mL
1/2 cup	chopped onion	125 mL
1	large sweet red pepper, chopped	1
1	clove garlic, minced	1
1-1/2 cups	chicken stock	375 mL
1	can (28 oz/796 mL) tomatoes, drained and chopped	1
1 cup	long-grain rice	250 mL
1 tsp	salt	5 mL
1/2 tsp	dried thyme	2 mL
	Pepper	
1 lb	large shrimp, peeled and deveined	500 g
1/2 lb	cooked ham, cut in thin strips	250 g
Dash	hot pepper sauce	Dash
	Chopped fresh parsley	

■ In large heavy saucepan, cook bacon over medium heat for about 5 minutes or until crisp; drain on paper towels and set aside.

■ Wipe out pan and melt butter; cook onion, red pepper and garlic for about 3 minutes or until tender. Stir in bacon, chicken stock, tomatoes, rice, salt, thyme, and pepper to taste. Bring to boil; reduce heat, cover and simmer for 20 minutes.

■ Add shrimp and cook for about 5 minutes or until shrimp are pink and tender and most of the liquid has been absorbed. Stir in ham and hot pepper sauce. Taste and adjust seasoning if necessary. Garnish with parsley. Makes about 4 servings.

Sole Fillets with Dill

Individually quick-frozen sole fillets are especially well suited to small households because you can thaw just the amount you need. Other firm white fish, either fresh or frozen, can be used in this recipe. Serve fillets with baked sweet potatoes or squash, and coleslaw made with cabbage and colorful sweet peppers.

4	sole fillets (about 1/2 lb/250 g)	4
1 tbsp	mayonnaise	15 mL
1/4 tsp	salt	1 mL
Pinch	pepper	Pinch
Half	slice toasted whole wheat bread	Half
2 tbsp	chopped fresh dill	25 mL
2 tsp	butter	10 mL
1	clove garlic	1
1 tsp	coarsely grated lemon rind	5 mL
2	lemon wedges	2

■ Pat fillets dry. Spread mayonnaise over broad half of each fillet. Season with salt and pepper.

■ In food processor, process toast into crumbs. Add dill, butter, garlic and lemon rind; process until garlic is finely minced. Sprinkle over seasoned half of fillets. Fold narrow end of fillet over crumb mixture to form roll. Arrange in greased shallow 8-inch (2 L) ovenproof dish.

■ Bake in 450°F (230°C) oven for 10 minutes or until fish flakes easily when tested with fork. Garnish with lemon. Makes 2 servings.

Poached Haddock with Plum Tomatoes

Use any white fish for this quick and easy main dish. Fresh fish is best, but frozen fillets work well, too.

1/4 cup	olive oil	50 mL
2	onions, chopped	2
2	carrots, thinly sliced	2
1	can (19 oz/540 mL) plum tomatoes (undrained)	1
1/2 cup	white wine	125 mL
1	large clove garlic, minced	1
	Salt and pepper	
4	haddock fillets or steaks (each 6 oz/175 g)	4
1/4 cup	chopped watercress	50 mL

■ In large skillet, heat oil over medium-high heat; cook onions and carrots, covered, until softened but not browned, about 2 minutes. Add tomatoes, wine, garlic, and salt and pepper to taste; bring to boil. Reduce heat to medium; cook for 3 minutes or until saucy.

■ Arrange fish in sauce; return to boil. Reduce heat to medium-low and simmer, covered, for 10 minutes per inch (2.5 cm) thickness or until fish flakes easily when tested with fork. Sprinkle with watercress. Serve immediately. Makes 4 servings.

Sole Fillets with Dill ▶

Suppertime Tuna Melt

Here's a delicious open-faced sandwich that pairs beautifully with a salad made of chunks of tomato, chopped celery and a jar (6 oz/170 mL) of marinated artichokes.

3/4 cup	mayonnaise	175 mL
4	pita breads	4
2	cans (each 6.5 oz/184 g) flaked tuna, drained	2
1/2 cup	chopped celery	125 mL
1/2 cup	minced dill pickle	125 mL
2	green onions, chopped	2
	Salt and pepper	
1 cup	shredded Cheddar cheese	250 mL

■ Spread 1 tbsp (15 mL) of the mayonnaise over each pita. Combine tuna, celery, pickle, onions, remaining mayonnaise, and salt and pepper to taste; spread over pitas. Sprinkle with cheese, covering as much area as possible. Broil on baking sheet 4 inches (10 cm) from heat for 3 minutes or until heated through and bubbling. Makes 4 servings.

Herbed Pasta-and-Seafood Stew

This is wonderful with fresh fish fillets, but if they are unavailable, use frozen fillets, such as sole, cod or haddock. Serve in large bowls with crusty bread.

1 lb	fish fillets	500 g
1	can (10 oz/284 mL) baby clams	1
1 tbsp	olive oil	15 mL
1 cup	chopped green onions	250 mL
1	large clove garlic, minced	1
1	can (28 oz/796 mL) tomatoes (undrained), chopped	1
3 cups	tomato juice	750 mL
1/2 cup	chopped fresh parsley	125 mL
1 tsp	grated lemon rind	5 mL
1/2 tsp	dried basil	2 mL
Pinch	hot pepper flakes	Pinch
1 cup	pasta shells or other small pasta	250 mL

■ Cut fish into 1-inch (2.5 cm) chunks. Drain clams, reserving juice; set aside.

■ In large heavy saucepan, heat oil over medium-high heat; cook onions and garlic until tender, about 2 minutes. Stir in tomatoes, tomato juice, reserved clam juice, parsley, lemon rind, basil and hot pepper flakes; cover and bring to boil.

■ Add pasta and reduce heat; simmer for 10 minutes or until fish flakes easily when tested with fork. Makes 4 servings.

Tuna-Broccoli Potatoes

These main-course potatoes make a nutritious supper that's easy on the budget and the cook. Accompany them with a simple green salad.

4	large baking potatoes	4
	Vegetable oil	
5 cups	broccoli florets (1 bunch)	1.25 L
1	can (6.5 oz/184 g) tuna, drained	1
1/4 cup	diced celery	50 mL
1/4 cup	chopped green onions	50 mL
1/2 cup	mayonnaise	125 mL
1/2 cup	sour cream	125 mL
1 tsp	Dijon mustard	5 mL
2 tbsp	butter, melted	25 mL
Pinch	cayenne pepper	Pinch
	Salt and black pepper	

■ Scrub potatoes and prick skins with fork; rub all over with oil. Bake in 425°F (220°C) oven for 45 to 55 minutes or until potatoes yield to gentle pressure.

■ Meanwhile, in large pot of boiling water, cook broccoli, uncovered, for 2 to 3 minutes or until tender-crisp. Drain and rinse under cold water; drain well and chop coarsely. Place in large bowl. Coarsely flake tuna; add to broccoli along with celery and onions. Stir together mayonnaise, sour cream and mustard; set aside.

■ Cut each potato in half lengthwise; carefully scoop out pulp leaving 1/4-inch (5 mm) thick shell. Brush skins with butter; place on baking sheet and keep warm.

■ In bowl, mash potato pulp; mix in broccoli mixture and 3/4 cup (175 mL) of the mayonnaise mixture. Stir in cayenne, and salt and pepper to taste. Stuff into potato skins, mounding tops. Return to oven and bake for 15 minutes or until steaming hot. Serve with remaining mayonnaise mixture spooned over each potato. Makes 4 servings.

Peanut Crunch Oven-Fried Fillets

An easy coating adds crunch to baked fish while keeping it moist inside.
Accompany the fillets with rice tossed with peas and creamy coleslaw.

1 cup	fine dry bread crumbs	250 mL
1/2 cup	finely chopped peanuts	125 mL
1/2 tsp	salt	2 mL
1/4 tsp	pepper	1 mL
2	eggs, beaten	2
4 tsp	vegetable oil	20 mL
1 lb	fish fillets	500 g

■ In shallow dish, combine bread crumbs, peanuts, salt and pepper. In small bowl, beat eggs with oil. Pat fish dry with paper towels.
■ Dip each fillet into egg mixture, then into crumbs; place on greased baking sheet. *(Recipe can be prepared to this point, covered and refrigerated for up to 6 hours.)* Bake, uncovered, in 450°F (230°C) oven for 6 minutes. Turn and bake for 1 to 3 minutes longer or until crispy and fish flakes easily when tested with fork. Makes 4 servings.

Microwave Parsley-and-Lemon Sole Roll-Ups

Sole fillets wrapped around a lemon-scented herb stuffing make fine company fare.

1 tbsp	butter	15 mL
1	onion, chopped	1
1	clove garlic, minced	1
1/2 cup	fresh bread crumbs	125 mL
1/3 cup	chopped fresh parsley	75 mL
2 tbsp	lemon juice	25 mL
1 tsp	grated lemon rind	5 mL
1/4 tsp	salt	1 mL
Pinch	pepper	Pinch
4	sole fillets (about 1 lb/500 g)	4

■ In 4-cup (1 L) microwaveable measure or bowl, microwave butter at High for 30 seconds or until melted. Add onion and garlic; microwave at High for 1 to 2 minutes or until softened, stirring once. Stir in bread crumbs, 1/4 cup (50 mL) of the parsley, 1 tbsp (15 mL) of the lemon juice, lemon rind, salt and pepper; spread evenly over fillets. Starting at narrow end, roll up fillets jelly-roll style; secure with toothpicks.

■ Arrange roll-ups in circle around outside of shallow microwaveable dish; sprinkle with remaining lemon juice. Cover and microwave at High for 4 minutes or until fish flakes easily when tested with fork. Sprinkle with remaining parsley. Makes 4 servings.

FAST MICROWAVE FISH STICKS
Transform a block of frozen fish into easy sticks. Microwave a 1-lb (500 g) frozen block at Defrost or Medium-Low (30%) for 2 to 3 minutes or just until fish can be cut with a knife. Cut crosswise into 8 even strips. Roll sticks in your favorite breading mixture. Arrange, spoke-fashion, on paper towel-lined microwaveable plate; microwave at High for 5 to 6 minutes or until fish flakes easily when tested with fork, rotating dish once.

Salmon Corn Cakes with Cucumber Dill Sauce

Just when you think there's nothing in the house for supper, a can of salmon and a bit of frozen corn come to the rescue.

3 tbsp	vegetable oil	50 mL
1	small onion, chopped	1
Half	sweet green pepper, diced	Half
1/2 cup	frozen corn kernels, thawed and patted dry	125 mL
1	clove garlic, minced	1
1	can (15.5 oz/439 g) pink salmon (undrained)	1
2 tbsp	chopped fresh parsley	25 mL
2 tbsp	lemon juice	25 mL
1	egg, lightly beaten	1
1/2 tsp	salt	2 mL
1/4 tsp	dried dillweed	1 mL
Pinch	black pepper	Pinch
Pinch	cayenne pepper	Pinch
1/3 cup	dry bread crumbs	75 mL
1/3 cup	cornmeal	75 mL
2 tbsp	butter	25 mL
	Cucumber Dill Sauce (recipe follows)	

■ In skillet, heat 1 tbsp (15 mL) of the oil over medium heat; cook onion, green pepper, corn and garlic for 5 minutes. Let cool slightly.

■ In large bowl, stir together salmon (mashing bones), parsley, lemon juice, egg, salt, dillweed, black and cayenne peppers and onion mixture. Stir in just enough bread crumbs to make firm but moist mixture.

■ Shape into 8 patties about 2-1/2 inches (6 cm) in diameter. Coat well with cornmeal. Cover with waxed paper and refrigerate for at least 30 minutes or for up to 6 hours.

■ In large skillet, heat butter and remaining oil over medium heat; cook patties, turning once, for 6 to 8 minutes or until crisp and golden brown. Serve hot with Cucumber Dill Sauce. Makes 4 servings.

CUCUMBER DILL SAUCE

2/3 cup	plain yogurt	150 mL
1/2 cup	shredded seeded peeled cucumber	125 mL
1 tbsp	snipped fresh dill (or 1/2 tsp/2 mL dried dillweed)	15 mL
1/2 tsp	granulated sugar	2 mL
	Salt	

■ In bowl, stir together yogurt, cucumber, dill, sugar, and salt to taste. Cover and refrigerate for up to 2 hours. Makes about 1 cup (250 mL).

Lemon-Baked Fish

Baking time depends on the thickness of fillets in this dish. Allow 10 minutes per inch (2.5 cm) of thickness.

1/2 tsp	grated lemon rind	2 mL
1 tbsp	lemon juice	15 mL
1 tbsp	vegetable oil	15 mL
2	cloves garlic, minced	2
1 lb	fish fillets	500 g
	Salt and pepper	

■ In small bowl, stir together lemon rind and juice, oil and garlic.

■ **Conventional method:** Arrange fillets in single layer in shallow baking dish; sprinkle with salt and pepper to taste. Brush lemon mixture over fish. Bake in 450°F (230°C) oven for 8 to 10 minutes or until fish is opaque and flakes easily when tested with fork.

■ **Microwave method:** Arrange fillets in round microwaveable dish with thickest parts toward outside. Sprinkle with salt and pepper to taste. Brush lemon mixture over fish. Cover with waxed paper and microwave at High for 4 to 6 minutes or until fish is opaque and flakes easily when tested with fork. Let stand, covered, for 5 minutes.

■ Makes 4 servings.

Packets of Fish Fillets with Snow Peas

Use any firm-textured fresh or thawed frozen fish such as haddock, cod or red snapper. Accompany this dish with Sesame Rice (see Cooking for Company, *p. 40).*

4	fish fillets (1 lb/500 g total)	4
1 tbsp	minced gingerroot (or 1/4 tsp/1 mL ground ginger)	15 mL
1 tbsp	soy sauce	15 mL
1	clove garlic, minced	1
3/4 cup	thinly sliced carrots	175 mL
3/4 cup	snow peas	175 mL
2 tbsp	chopped green onion (white and green parts)	25 mL

■ Cut four 12-inch (30 cm) squares of parchment paper or foil; fold each into triangle, then open into square again. Arrange each fillet, tucking ends under, on one side of each fold. Combine gingerroot, soy sauce and garlic; drizzle over fish. Sprinkle each with carrots, snow peas and onion.

■ Fold into triangle again; fold edges over to seal tightly. On baking sheet, bake packages in 450°F (230°C) oven for 10 to 12 minutes or until fish flakes easily when tested with fork and vegetables are tender-crisp. Makes 4 servings.

Marinated Artichoke and Tomato Pizza with Cornmeal Crust

Why not try pizza on the barbecue? It's a great summertime twist to an old favorite. If provolone cheese is unavailable, simply double the mozzarella.

3/4 cup	whole wheat flour	175 mL
1/2 cup	all-purpose flour	125 mL
1/2 cup	cornmeal	125 mL
1 tsp	baking powder	5 mL
1/2 tsp	baking soda	2 mL
1/2 tsp	salt	2 mL
1/2 tsp	dried basil	2 mL
3/4 cup	plain yogurt	175 mL
2 tbsp	vegetable oil	25 mL

TOPPING		
3	tomatoes	3
1	jar (6 oz/170 mL) marinated artichokes	1
1/3 cup	black olives	75 mL
2	green onions	2
1 cup	shredded mozzarella cheese	250 mL
1 cup	shredded provolone cheese	250 mL
1/4 cup	finely shredded fresh basil (optional)	50 mL

■ In large bowl, stir together whole wheat and all-purpose flours, cornmeal, baking powder, baking soda, salt and basil. Combine yogurt with oil; pour over flour mixture, stirring with fork. On lightly floured surface, knead dough lightly into ball. Cover and let stand while preparing topping.

■ **Topping:** Meanwhile, core, halve and seed tomatoes. Cut into wedges; halve each wedge. Drain and halve artichokes. Halve and pit olives. Slice green ends of onions diagonally, reserving white portion for another use. In bowl, toss together shredded mozzarella and provolone.

■ On lightly floured surface, roll out dough to 1/4-inch (5 mm) thickness. Transfer to greased 12-inch (30 cm) pizza pan. Sprinkle 1-1/2 cups (375 mL) of the cheese over crust right to edge. Top with tomatoes, artichokes and olives. Sprinkle with remaining cheese and green onions.

■ **Barbecue method:** Place pizza pan on grill 4 to 6 inches (10 to 15 cm) from medium-hot coals or on medium-high setting. Grill, covered, for 10 to 15 minutes, rotating pan every 3 minutes, or until crust is crisp, bottom is golden and cheese is melted. Sprinkle with basil (if using).

■ **Oven method:** Place inverted baking sheet on bottom rack of 500°F (260°C) oven for 2 minutes. Meanwhile, roll out dough as above and place on pizza pan. Place pan on inverted baking sheet and bake for 5 to 7 minutes or until crust is firm and beginning to brown. Add topping ingredients; bake for 10 minutes or until crust is browned and cheese is melted.

■ Makes 4 to 6 servings.

Broccoli and Cheddar Frittata

For a light meal, serve this egg dish hot or at room temperature with crusty bread and carrot sticks.

3 cups	broccoli florets, cut in bite-size pieces	750 mL
2 tbsp	olive oil	25 mL
2	onions, chopped	2
6	eggs	6
1/3 cup	milk	75 mL
1/2 tsp	salt	2 mL
Pinch	pepper	Pinch
1 cup	diced Cheddar cheese (1/4 lb/125 g)	250 mL

■ In large pot of boiling water, cook broccoli for 3 to 4 minutes or just until tender-crisp. Drain and refresh under cold water; drain again and pat dry. Set aside.

■ In 10-inch (25 cm) ovenproof skillet, heat oil over medium heat; cook onions for 3 to 5 minutes or until softened. Remove pan from heat and arrange broccoli over onions. Whisk together eggs, milk, salt and pepper; gently pour over broccoli. Scatter cheese over top.

■ Return pan to medium-low heat; cook, covered, for 15 to 20 minutes or until almost set but still moist on surface. Broil for about 2 minutes or until lightly browned. Cut into wedges to serve. Makes 4 servings.

Spanish Rice and Lentil Pilaf

This meatless dish can be made a day ahead and reheated just before serving. Accompany the pilaf with a Waldorf salad for a satisfying supper.

2 cups	vegetable stock	500 mL
1/2 cup	green lentils, rinsed	125 mL
1/2 cup	brown rice	125 mL
1	can (19 oz/540 mL) stewed tomatoes	1
1-1/2 tsp	dried basil	7 mL
	Salt and pepper	
1 cup	shredded Cheddar cheese	250 mL

■ **Conventional method:** In saucepan, combine stock, lentils, rice, tomatoes and basil; bring to boil. Reduce heat, cover and simmer for 50 to 60 minutes or until lentils and rice are tender and most of the liquid is absorbed.

■ **Microwave method:** In 12-cup (3 L) microwaveable casserole, combine stock, lentils, rice, tomatoes and basil; cover and microwave at High for 8 to 10 minutes or until boiling. Microwave at Medium (50%) for 40 to 45 minutes or until lentils and rice are tender and most of the liquid is absorbed. Let stand, covered, for 5 minutes.

■ **Both methods:** Season with salt and pepper to taste. Spoon onto plates and sprinkle each with cheese. Makes 4 servings.

Open-Faced Asparagus Omelette

For a lighter dish, use only six eggs along with four egg whites. Serve it with rolls or scones and a marinated beet salad with green onions.

2 tbsp	butter	25 mL
2 tbsp	olive oil	25 mL
3 cups	sliced mushrooms	750 mL
1	clove garlic, minced	1
8	eggs	8
1/3 cup	chopped fresh parsley	75 mL
1/4 tsp	pepper	1 mL
1	can (12 oz/341 mL) green asparagus tips, drained	1
1 cup	shredded mozzarella cheese	250 mL
1/4 cup	freshly grated Parmesan cheese	50 mL

■ In large skillet with ovenproof handle, heat 1 tbsp (15 mL) each of the butter and oil over high heat; cook mushrooms and garlic, stirring often, for about 2 minutes or until mushrooms are softened. With slotted spoon, remove to bowl and set aside.

■ Drain liquid from skillet; heat remaining butter and oil over medium heat, swirling to coat pan. Combine eggs, parsley and pepper; pour into skillet. Cover and cook over medium-low heat for 5 to 7 minutes or until top is almost set. Sprinkle with mushroom mixture; arrange asparagus like spokes of wheel on top. Sprinkle with mozzarella, then Parmesan. Broil until cheese melts and is lightly browned.

Makes 4 servings.

Baked Italian Beans

Simple and easy, this nutritious casserole is packed with the robust flavors you associate with good old-fashioned spaghetti.

2 tbsp	vegetable oil	25 mL
2	carrots, coarsely chopped	2
2	stalks celery, coarsely chopped	2
2	cloves garlic, minced	2
1	onion, coarsely chopped	1
1	sweet green pepper, diced	1
1	can (28 oz/796 mL) tomatoes (undrained)	1
1	can (5-1/2 oz/156 mL) tomato paste	1
1 tsp	each dried oregano and basil	5 mL
Pinch	each hot pepper flakes and granulated sugar	Pinch
1/2 cup	freshly grated Parmesan cheese	125 mL
	Salt	
1	can (19 oz/540 mL) white kidney beans, drained	1
1	can (19 oz/540 mL) chick-peas, drained	1
1-1/2 cups	shredded mozzarella cheese	375 mL
1 cup	fresh bread crumbs	250 mL
1/4 cup	chopped fresh parsley	50 mL
2 tbsp	butter, melted	25 mL

■ In large saucepan, heat oil over medium heat; cook carrots, celery, garlic, onion and green pepper until softened, about 7 minutes.

■ Stir in tomatoes, tomato paste, 1 tomato paste can of water, oregano, basil, hot pepper flakes, sugar and 2 tbsp (25 mL) of the Parmesan cheese. Taste and season with salt if desired. Bring to boil; reduce heat and simmer, uncovered and stirring often, for 20 minutes or until slightly thickened. Stir in kidney beans and chick-peas; cook for 15 minutes. Taste and adjust seasoning.

■ Transfer to greased 13- × 9-inch (3 L) baking dish; sprinkle with mozzarella. Combine remaining Parmesan cheese, bread crumbs, parsley and butter; sprinkle over mozzarella. *(Recipe can be prepared to this point, covered and refrigerated for up to 24 hours. Let stand at room temperature for 30 minutes before heating.)*

■ Bake in 375°F (190°C) oven for 20 to 30 minutes or until bubbling. Makes 4 to 6 servings.

Vegetable Frittata

This dish is a bit like a crustless quiche or soufflé. For a more golden appearance, run it under the broiler for two to three minutes after baking.

6	eggs	6
1/4 cup	skim milk	50 mL
1/4 tsp	pepper	1 mL
1 cup	cubed whole wheat bread	250 mL
1 cup	shredded low-fat mozzarella or Swiss cheese	250 mL
2 oz	cream cheese, cubed	50 g
1 tbsp	vegetable oil	15 mL
1	onion, chopped	1
1 cup	chopped zucchini	250 mL
1 cup	chopped mushrooms	250 mL
1	sweet red or green pepper, chopped	1
2	cloves garlic, minced	2
1/2 tsp	dried oregano	2 mL
Pinch	crushed hot pepper flakes	Pinch
2	tomatoes, thinly sliced	2
1/4 cup	freshly grated Parmesan cheese	50 mL

■ In large bowl, whisk together eggs, milk and pepper; stir in bread, mozzarella and cream cheese. Set aside.

■ In 10-inch (25 cm) ovenproof skillet, heat oil over medium-high heat; sauté onion, zucchini, mushrooms, red pepper, garlic, oregano and hot pepper flakes for 2 to 3 minutes or until softened. Remove from heat; pour in egg mixture and mix well.

■ Arrange tomatoes over top; sprinkle with Parmesan. Bake in 375°F (190°C) oven for 25 minutes or until egg mixture is set and golden. Cut into wedges to serve. Makes 4 to 6 servings.

Fettuccine Primavera with Toasted Almonds

Toss this vegetarian dish together and serve it with crusty French bread for a quick, satisfying meal. Instead of broccoli, here's an opportunity to try a new green cauliflower, as we did for our photograph.

2 cups	broccoli florets	500 mL
2 cups	cauliflower florets	500 mL
1 cup	asparagus or green bean pieces	250 mL
1 lb	fresh fettuccine (or 3/4 lb/375 g dried)	500 g
1/4 cup	olive oil	50 mL
1	onion, chopped	1
1	carrot, chopped	1
1	small sweet red pepper, chopped	1
4	cloves garlic, chopped	4
1/2 cup	vegetable stock or water	125 mL
3 tbsp	chopped fresh basil	50 mL
1/4 tsp	pepper	1 mL
1/2 cup	freshly grated Parmesan cheese	125 mL
1/2 cup	toasted slivered almonds*	125 mL

■ Steam broccoli, cauliflower and asparagus for 5 to 8 minutes or until tender-crisp. Meanwhile, in large saucepan of boiling salted water, cook fresh fettuccine for 5 to 7 minutes, dried for 12 to 15 minutes, or until tender but firm. Drain well.

■ Meanwhile, in large skillet, heat oil over medium-high heat; sauté onion for 3 to 5 minutes or until golden brown. Add carrot, red pepper and garlic; sauté for 2 to 3 minutes or until vegetables are tender-crisp. Add to drained pasta along with broccoli mixture, stock, basil and pepper. Toss with Parmesan. Arrange on serving platter; sprinkle with almonds. Makes 4 servings.

*To toast almonds, bake on baking sheet in 375°F (190°C) oven for 5 to 8 minutes or until golden brown.

One-Pot Macaroni and Cheddar

Just as quick to make as commercial macaroni dinners, this meal will really please the kids with its chunky bites of wieners. For a vegetarian meal, omit wieners or use tofu wieners. Serve with crisp celery sticks and radishes.

2 cups	elbow macaroni (1/2 lb/250 g)	500 mL
1-1/2 cups	thinly sliced carrots	375 mL
2 cups	milk	500 mL
2 tbsp	all-purpose flour	25 mL
1 tbsp	Dijon mustard	15 mL
4	wieners, sliced	4
2 tbsp	butter	25 mL
2 cups	shredded Cheddar cheese (8 oz/250 g)	500 mL
4	green onions, chopped	4
	Salt and pepper	

■ In large saucepan of boiling salted water, cook macaroni for 5 minutes. Add carrots; cook for 4 to 5 minutes or until pasta and carrots are tender but firm. Drain; set aside.

■ In same saucepan, whisk together milk, flour and mustard; cook over medium-high heat, whisking, for 2 to 3 minutes or until thickened and smooth. Reduce heat to medium; cook for 1 minute longer. Stir in pasta, carrots, wieners and butter; cook, stirring, for 2 to 3 minutes or until heated through. Stir in cheese and onions; cook for 1 minute or until cheese melts. Season with salt and pepper to taste. Makes 4 servings.

Cheesy Beef Pasta

If you'd like more vegetables, add 1/4 cup (50 mL) frozen corn, peas or carrots along with the tomatoes.

1 lb	lean ground beef	500 g
1	onion	1
1	clove garlic, minced	1
1	sweet green pepper, chopped	1
1 tsp	dried basil	5 mL
1/2 tsp	dried thyme	2 mL
1	can (28 oz/796 mL) crushed tomatoes	1
1 cup	water	250 mL
2 cups	rotini pasta	500 mL
1/4 tsp	each salt and sugar	1 mL
Pinch	pepper	Pinch
1 cup	shredded mozzarella cheese (1/4 lb/125 g)	250 mL

■ In large nonstick skillet, cook beef over high heat, stirring, for 3 to 5 minutes or until no longer pink. Pour off all but 1 tbsp (15 mL) of fat. Cook onion, garlic, green pepper, basil and thyme, stirring, for 2 minutes.

■ Stir in tomatoes and water; bring to boil. Add pasta and reduce heat to simmer; cover partially and cook, stirring frequently, for about 15 minutes or until pasta is tender. Stir in salt, sugar and pepper. Remove from heat. Sprinkle with mozzarella. Cover and let stand until cheese has melted. Makes 4 servings.

Pasta Toss with Spinach and Pepperoni

Here's a light, fast way for the family to enjoy spinach — even if it's not the kids' favorite food. Serve with crusty bread and sliced tomatoes or skillet-warmed cherry tomatoes.

3/4 lb	pasta shells or penne	375 g
1/3 cup	olive oil	75 mL
3	cloves garlic, minced	3
3	green onions, chopped	3
1/2 cup	fine dry bread crumbs	125 mL
1/4 lb	pepperoni, thinly sliced	125 g
1	pkg (10 oz/284 g) fresh spinach, chopped	1
2 tsp	grated lemon rind	10 mL
1/2 cup	freshly grated Parmesan cheese	125 mL
	Salt and pepper	

■ In large pot of boiling salted water, cook pasta for 9 to 12 minutes or until tender but firm. Drain; return to pot.

■ Meanwhile, in skillet, heat 2 tbsp (25 mL) of the oil over medium-high heat; cook garlic and onions, stirring, for 1 minute or until softened. Add bread crumbs and pepperoni; cook, stirring, for 2 to 3 minutes or until crumbs are golden.

■ Remove from heat; stir in spinach and lemon rind. Add to pasta along with Parmesan and remaining oil; toss well. Season with salt and pepper to taste. Makes 4 servings.

Fall Vegetables and Fusilli

Enjoy our comfy pasta and chick-pea casserole as a vegetarian supper or for lunch. For a nonvegetarian version, replace vegetable stock with chicken stock and add chopped smoked turkey, ham, pastrami or chunks of drained salmon or tuna.

3 cups	fusilli (about 1/2 lb/250 g)	750 mL
1/4 cup	butter	50 mL
1 cup	chopped onions	250 mL
4	cloves garlic, minced	4
1-1/2 cups	diced carrots	375 mL
1 cup	chopped celery	250 mL
2 cups	quartered mushrooms	500 mL
2 cups	cubed zucchini	500 mL
1	large sweet red pepper, diced	1
1/4 cup	all-purpose flour	50 mL
2 tsp	dry mustard	10 mL
2 tsp	dried thyme or basil	10 mL
1-1/2 tsp	salt	7 mL
1/2 tsp	pepper	2 mL
2 cups	milk	500 mL
1-1/2 cups	vegetable stock	375 mL
1	can (19 oz/540 mL) chick-peas, drained	1
2 cups	shredded Cheddar cheese	500 mL
1-1/2 cups	soft bread crumbs	375 mL
1/2 cup	minced fresh parsley	125 mL

■ In large pot of boiling salted water, cook fusilli until tender but firm, about 10 minutes. Drain and rinse under cold water; set aside.

■ Meanwhile, in large heavy saucepan, melt butter over medium heat; cook onions, garlic, carrots and celery for 5 minutes, stirring. Add mushrooms, zucchini and red pepper; cook for about 5 minutes or until softened.

■ Stir in flour, mustard, thyme, salt and pepper; cook for 2 minutes, stirring. Gradually stir in milk and stock; bring to simmer and cook, stirring, for 5 minutes or until thickened. Add chick-peas and fusilli. Taste and adjust seasoning. Transfer to 13- × 9-inch (3 L) baking dish. *(Recipe can be prepared to this point, cooled, covered and refrigerated for up to 1 day or frozen for up to 2 months. Thaw before continuing and add 10 minutes to baking time.)*

■ Toss together cheese, bread crumbs and parsley; sprinkle over casserole. Bake in 375°F (190°C) oven for about 45 minutes or until crusty on top and bubbling. Makes about 8 servings.

Zesty Beef and Tomato Sauce

A touch of cinnamon sparks up a traditional favorite. For a change from spaghetti, serve this thick sauce over rigatoni, penne or rotini, using 3/4 lb (375 g) dried pasta. Pass 1/2 cup (125 mL) freshly grated Parmesan cheese separately.

2 tbsp	vegetable oil	25 mL
1 lb	ground beef	500 g
2 tbsp	butter or vegetable oil	25 mL
2 cups	diced mushrooms	500 mL
2	small onions, chopped	2
1/4 cup	chopped carrot	50 mL
2	cans (each 19 oz/540 mL) tomatoes	2
1 cup	water	250 mL
1/4 cup	tomato paste	50 mL
1/2 tsp	each salt, pepper, granulated sugar and dried basil	2 mL
Pinch	cinnamon	Pinch
1/4 cup	minced fresh parsley	50 mL

■ In large skillet, heat oil over medium-high heat; cook beef, breaking up pieces, for about 6 minutes or until no longer pink. Using slotted spoon, remove beef and set aside. Pour off fat.

■ In same skillet, melt butter over medium heat; cook mushrooms, onion and carrot until softened, about 6 minutes. Return meat to skillet.

■ Add tomatoes, crushing into small pieces with fork. Stir in water, tomato paste, salt, pepper, sugar, basil and cinnamon; bring to boil. Reduce heat and simmer, uncovered and stirring often, for about 30 minutes or until thickened. Taste and adjust seasoning. Stir in parsley. Makes 8 servings.

Lasagna Roll-Ups

This is a make-ahead casserole with the wonderful flavors of pizza and spaghetti all in one.

8	lasagna noodles	8
6 cups	(approx) Zesty Beef and Tomato Sauce (recipe above)	1.5 L
1-1/2 cups	shredded mozzarella cheese	375 mL
1/4 cup	freshly grated Parmesan cheese	50 mL

■ In large saucepan of boiling salted water, cook lasagna until tender but firm; drain and rinse with cold water. Set aside.

■ Spread about 3/4 cup (175 mL) sauce in greased 11- × 7-inch (2 L) baking dish. Spread about 1/2 cup (125 mL) sauce on each lasagna noodle. Carefully roll up and place seam side down in dish. Top with remaining sauce. Cover and bake in 350°F (180°C) oven for 45 minutes or until hot and bubbling.

■ Sprinkle with mozzarella and Parmesan; bake for 5 to 10 minutes or until cheese melts and top is lightly browned. Makes 4 to 6 servings.

Mushroom Lasagna

This vegetarian lasagna can be lightened up by substituting low-fat mozzarella and cottage cheese. Omit olive oil and sautéing step. Instead, simmer vegetables with tomatoes.

2 tbsp	olive oil	25 mL
1	small onion, finely chopped	1
1	clove garlic, minced	1
1	stalk celery, finely chopped	1
3/4 lb	mushrooms, thinly sliced	375 g
Half	sweet red pepper, finely chopped	Half
2 cups	canned plum tomatoes	500 mL
1/2 tsp	each dried thyme, oregano and basil	2 mL
	Salt and pepper	
4	lasagna noodles	4
1-1/2 cups	cottage cheese	375 mL
1-1/2 cups	shredded mozzarella cheese	375 mL
1/4 cup	freshly grated Parmesan cheese	50 mL

■ In saucepan, heat oil over medium heat; cook onion, garlic and celery for 3 minutes or until onion is softened. Stir in mushrooms and red pepper; cook, stirring occasionally, for 5 minutes or until liquid has evaporated.

■ Add tomatoes, thyme, oregano and basil; bring to boil. Reduce heat and simmer, uncovered, for 15 to 20 minutes or until thickened.

Season with salt and pepper to taste.

■ In large saucepan of lightly salted boiling water, cook noodles until tender but firm; drain and rinse under cold water. Spread on damp tea towel.

■ **Assembly:** Spread one-quarter of the mushroom mixture in 8-inch (2 L) square baking or lasagna dish. Top with layer of noodles, cutting to fit dish and using ends to fill spaces. Spread with half of the cottage cheese; sprinkle with half of the mozzarella. Spread another quarter of the mushroom mixture over top.

■ Repeat layering with remaining ingredients, ending with mushroom mixture. Sprinkle with Parmesan. Bake in 350°F (180°C) oven for 35 minutes or until heated through and bubbling around sides. Makes about 6 servings.

Credits

Recipes in THE CANADIAN LIVING COOKING COLLECTION have been created by the *Canadian Living* Test Kitchen and by the following food writers from across Canada: **Elizabeth Baird, Karen Brown, Joanna Burkhard, James Chatto, Diane Clement, David Cohlmeyer, Pam Collacott, Bonnie Baker Cowan, Pierre Dubrulle, Eileen Dwillies, Nancy Enright, Carol Ferguson, Margaret Fraser, Susan Furlan, Anita Goldberg, Barb Holland, Patricia Jamieson, Arlene Lappin, Anne Lindsay, Lispeth Lodge, Mary McGrath, Susan Mendelson, Bernard Meyer, Beth Moffatt, Rose Murray, Iris Raven, Gerry Shikatani, Jill Snider, Kay Spicer, Linda Stephen, Bonnie Stern, Lucy Waverman, Carol White, Ted Whittaker** and **Cynny Willet.**

The full-color photographs throughout are by Canada's leading food photographers, including **Fred Bird, Doug Bradshaw, Christopher Campbell, Nino D'Angelo, Frank Grant, Michael Kohn, Suzanne McCormick, Claude Noel, John Stephens** and **Mike Visser.**

Editorial and Production Staff: Hugh Brewster, Susan Barrable, Catherine Fraccaro, Wanda Nowakowska, Sandra L. Hall, Beverley Renahan and Bernice Eisenstein.

Index

LOOK FOR THESE
BESTSELLING COOKBOOKS
FROM *CANADIAN LIVING*

The most trusted name in Canadian cooking

The Everyday DASH Diet Guide

The 4 Weeks Meal Plan to Lose Weight, Boost Metabolism, and Live a Healthy Life

Charles Kelso

Table of Contents

Disclaimer Notice

Get an Audio Book for FREE!

Don't have an Audible account?

Sign up and get "The Everyday DASH Diet Guide" audio book for FREE!

http://bit.ly/kelso-dash-diet

Introduction
Basics of DASH Dieting

DASH is an acronym that stands for Dietary Approaches to Stop Hypertension. There is a reason that this diet has been ranked consistently as the best heart-healthy diet in the world. It's not some fad that this week's Internet expert is trying to pass off as some kind of magic. The DASH diet follows healthy eating and is more of a lifestyle choice than it is a diet.

In fact, if you can consistently follow this plan for four weeks, then you'll find that the foods you eat taste much better. One of the things that shocked me the most about this new lifestyle was just how many wasteful calories I was consuming before. If I try eating those foods now, they taste like–well--junk! Clean eating provides a much wider palette of flavors. The problem is that we're in a world filled with unhealthy choices, but we're so used to those artificial flavors that real food tastes strange. You will discover that, once you break that cycle, all of those unhealthy choices seem much less appealing.

The DASH diet provides a long-term solution for your health, so if you're looking for a quick fix, or one of those fad dieting schemes, then you should probably look elsewhere. But if you're looking for a long-term solution that will change your life for the better, then this is the perfect book for you.

We mostly hear the praise for the DASH diet's positive effects on blood pressure, but the change to whole, fresh foods is healthy in pretty much every way imaginable. That's why its ranking is so consistent.

Dieting plans that demand extreme calorie restrictions have no scientific evidence that they are efficient. They are just something that happened to work for one person, and so that person decided

to tell the world about their perfect diet. This book will show you an efficient plan laid out with manageable changes that are founded on the principle of eating healthier foods. It's not about starving yourself or making extreme choices. It's about eating in the way that your body wants you to eat.

What Are the Benefits of the DASH Diet?

The DASH diet was developed specifically to help people suffering from high blood pressure, so naturally, it's heavily promoted by the National Heart, Lung, and Blood Institute. The food options are quite vast, putting an emphasis on whole foods like vegetables and fruit, fat-free dairy products, lean meats, and whole grains. It also eliminates processed foods, simple sugars, and packaged snacks. It's also encouraged that you limit red meats.

Processed foods do not taste that great anyway. You just think they do now because your palate is out of balance. Once you clean up your eating habits, you'll wonder why you ever ate those foods in the first place!

The DASH diet also limits sodium intake, which can give you an edge over hypertension and also help you to lose weight. This is a great choice for individuals who might have a family history of heart disease or those at risk of type-2 diabetes.

Therefore, you have two choices here:

Standard DASH Diet: Limits sodium intake to 2,300 milligrams per day.

Lower-Sodium DASH Diet: Limit sodium intake to 1,500 per day.

On average, the DASH dieting plan will include the following foods on a daily basis:

- ➢ 8 servings of whole grains
- ➢ 6 servings of meat

- ➤ 5 servings of vegetables

- ➤ 4 servings of fruit

- ➤ 2-3 servings of fat-free dairy products

- ➤ 2 servings of oils

Some of the daily goals will include:

- ➤ Fat should never be more than 27% of your calorie intake, with saturated fat making up no more than 6%.

- ➤ Protein should be 18% of your calorie intake.

- ➤ Carbohydrates should be 55% of your total calorie intake

- ➤ Never consume more than 150 mg of cholesterol

- ➤ Consume at least 30 grams of fiber

As you can see, this is a lifestyle choice. It doesn't rely on giving up one area of nutrition to boost another. It's not based on some fad with no scientific evidence to support it. It simply involves making better food choices and paying attention to what you're putting into your body.

If you are looking to lose weight, then you might need to restrict calories in the beginning so that your body can burn off some of those excess calories being stored. Extreme cuts do not work–they send your body into starvation mode, which actually slows the burn of calories.

For example, a lot of diets will demand that you cut your calorie intake to some lowball number (like 1,200) immediately. But you will actually lose weight faster if you lower your intake in increments like this:

- ➤ **Week 1:** 2,000 calories

- ➢ **Week 2:** 1,800 calories

- ➢ **Week 3:** 1,600 calories

- ➢ **Week 4:** 1,400 calories

- ➢ **Week 5:** 1,200 calories

Another of the major advantages of the DASH diet is that it limits salt, saturated fat, and cholesterol. All three of those contribute to heart disease, so by removing them, your heart health will improve drastically. Then you boost it even further by introducing heart-healthy nutrients like fiber.

What you consume is the most important aspect of your health. Contrary to what I hear many so-called Internet "experts" say, exercise does not fix everything. You cannot out exercise a bad diet. My point is that being mindful of what you consume is the most important aspect of leading a healthier lifestyle. Sure, you can incorporate other things into your overall plan, and we will be exploring a few of those in this book, but it still always comes back to consumption.

Research-Backed Benefits of DASH Dieting

While the DASH diet is mostly promoted as a lifestyle change for people looking to lower their blood pressure, it's a great choice for anyone looking to adopt a healthier lifestyle. It puts an emphasis on consuming whole foods in moderate portions, so it will automatically lead to a better overall lifestyle. With that said, here are some of the benefits.

It's a Long-Term Solution
Whole foods taste so much better than their processed counterparts. Since you are not forced to make extreme cuts, the long-term potential is actually easy to achieve. In fact, once you

start living this lifestyle, you will not even want to go back to processed foods.

It's Heart-Healthy

Dash dieting lowers blood pressure and boosts your cholesterol health in ways that no other diet can. Don't take my word for it. There have been several studies done to prove this point. A study published by the *American Journal of Clinical Nutrition* revealed that individuals who stuck to the DASH diet experienced lower blood pressure and lowered their LDL (bad cholesterol) levels. [1]

Reduce Risk of Specific Diseases

A stronger heart will improve your overall health like kidney function, blood sugar, and even your eye health. It can also reduce your risk of stroke. Since it's a long-term lifestyle choice, you will experience these benefits for the rest of your life.

Helps Manage Type 2 Diabetes

If you already suffer from, or are at risk for, Type 2 Diabetes, then the DASH diet will help you manage this disease. According to *'Current Hypertension Reports,* combining this dieting plan with an exercise regimen will result in a reduction in insulin resistance, which is the main symptom of Type 2 Diabetes. [2]

Better Overall Nutrition

When you start putting an emphasis on eating whole foods and ditch processed foods, your body will get far more nutrients. Your body is designed to run on whole foods, but society has brainwashed you into thinking that processed foods are better. Again, after a few weeks, you will start to wonder how in the world you ever ate those types of unhealthy foods.

---

[1] https://www.ncbi.nlm.nih.gov/pmc/articles/PMC4733264/
[2] https://www.ncbi.nlm.nih.gov/pmc/articles/PMC3767170/

Can Lead to Weight Loss

While the DASH diet isn't designed for weight loss per se, living a healthier lifestyle makes losing weight so much easier. Plus, I'm going to show you some amazing tricks to add to this lifestyle change that will make weight loss a breeze! Additionally, you will learn to keep close track of your calorie intake so you'll be able to better manage weight loss.

One of the downsides of the DASH diet is that it's difficult to adjust to consuming the required amount of fiber. It's hard on some people's body, so it's best to slowly add foods with high fiber to your diet. Don't try to do everything at once. Lay out a plan, and then follow it. If you start to feel bloated, then try drinking more water.

Overall, this book is going to show you how to get your health back on track by making some amazing changes. Then I will lay out a four-week meal plan, along with recipes, at the end of this book. The goal is to make this journey to a healthier life as easy as possible.

Chapter 1
Three Easy Changes You Can Make Right Now

There is a reason why DASH dieting is recommended by a lot of experts in the health industry. It's an easy way to ensure a healthy lifestyle. This book will walk you through the entire process. Naturally, the best place to start is with the easiest choices, so let's look at a few of those now.

Make Gradual Changes

Gradually make healthier choices to your dieting plan. You're not going to change your entire way of life in a single day, so plan for small changes that gradually move you in the right direction. The reason that so many people fail is that they try to make changes that are unrealistic. Rather than setting yourself up for failure, start small.

- ➢ Make one or two small changes every day.

- ➢ Replace an unhealthy choice with fresh veggies for lunch.

- ➢ Add a serving of fruit to your meal, or better yet, replace a snack with fruit.

- ➢ Swap to whole grain bread.

- ➢ Switch to whole grain, no added sugar cereal.

- ➢ Rather than filling your plate with food, opt for a smaller portion.

- Experiment with healthy recipes by adding a new one every week. Write down your favorites, and slowly replace less healthy meal plans with those healthy ones.

- If you love ice cream, choose low-fat frozen yogurt instead.

- Replace sugary drinks with club soda or water. This one is a huge step!

- When you get a sweet tooth, opt for fruit over processed snacks. You can eat canned fruit as long as it's not packed in syrup. Look at the label.

The DASH diet is focused on whole grains, vegetables, and fruit, so you need to gradually incorporate those into your lifestyle. Additionally, you will also need to start reducing your food portions. Instead of just piling food onto your plate, start measuring out one serving of each food.

Make sure that you slowly incorporate fiber into your diet. Adding too much fiber too quickly will make you feel bloated and can lead to diarrhea. These symptoms are not unhealthy. It's your body detoxifying itself, but it could really test your patience. We want this to be easy.

If you are lactose intolerant, then you can opt for lactose-free products rather than dairy. If you're allergic to nuts, then choose seeds or legumes instead. This is not some super strict plan like so many others before it. The idea is to make a lifestyle change. Those take more time and commitment but become much easier the longer you do it. Fad diets get

more difficult as you continue, which is why they fail more often than not.

Limit Meat Consumption

If you are an avid consumer of meat, then you should start cutting back on it. Try only eating two servings of meat per day. This actually has two major advantages. One is that it's a healthy choice. Second is that meatless meals are often much more budget-friendly. Try going meatless once or twice a week–basing your diet around plant-based proteins like beans, lentils, vegetables, and whole grains.

Plant-based meals are loaded with vitamins and important nutrients. Did you know that vegetarians consume fewer calories on average than meat eaters? Now, I'm not saying that you need to start living a vegan lifestyle, only that you make a small change to the way you look at food. You do not need more than two servings of meat per day, especially when there are so many healthy choices out there.

How much protein is enough? You only need 50 grams of protein per day at the most, so cutting back on meat is not going to hurt you.

Additionally, you can replace fatty meats (red meat) with leaner meats like fish and poultry. Again, don't do this all at once. Start by reducing your meat servings per day by one serving until you work your way down to two per day. Then after a few weeks, you can start to add in meatless days until you are at two.

Substitute Healthy Desserts

You should immediately replace all of your sugary, processed dessert choices with dried, fresh, or canned fruits. Fruit is sweet, but is loaded with other healthy nutrients. For example, most processed desserts do not have Vitamin A or Vitamin C, both of which are essential vitamins for the body.

Fruit also provides nutrients like fiber and folic acid. So next time you get a sweet tooth, bypass those baked goods, and try eating a piece of fruit. In fact, berries will give you the added bonus of an energy boost. It's a neat trick that nutritionists use to help their clients with that afternoon energy crash.

Nutrients provided by fruit are so important to your body that they simply cannot be ignored. The easiest way to incorporate them into your daily life is to use them as a dessert treat. Here are some of the many benefits of fruit:

> Diets rich in fruit can reduce the risk for stroke, cardiovascular disease, and Type-2 diabetes.

> Fruit-rich diets can reduce the risk of certain cancer.

> Fruits promote phytochemicals, which will promote and maintain your overall health.

You only have to consume one to two cups of fruit each day to reap in the benefits, so making this small change will probably get your health on the right track.

Reduce Oils

This one is actually quite easy. Reduce the oils that you use when cooking by half. Almost everyone overuses oils for cooking, so this reduction is quite easy. It will improve the quality of your food. Oil is bad for two important reasons:

#1: Oil is Pure Fat
Even olive oil is pure fat, so you should use as little as possible. It doesn't offer any real nutritional value, even though it's a good alternative. Marketers love to try to convince you otherwise, but you are basically consuming concentrated calories. My point is that we all use way too much oil because it's easy to do. That's why it's so important to measure it.

#2: Oil Lacks Nutrients
Again, it's just a concentrated mixture of calories. It has no vitamins or minerals that help you at all. All healthy elements are left out when it's processed. However, you still need to use it in order to cook efficiently. That's why we use olive oil in our recipes. The key is to use as little as possible. With that said, you can also use raw and cold-pressed oils since a lot of the nutrients are preserved. Again, these are simple changes that require minimal effort.

Increase Your Dairy Intake

Today's society pushes sugary beverages at us like they are the best thing in the world! But they are actually the opposite. Marketing focuses on the emotions attached to these sugary drinks to blind us from the fact that they are poison. You are going to have to get rid of these drinks if you plan on living a healthy life. There is no wiggle-room here.

So let's make this easier on you by replacing all sodas and other sugar-filled drinks with fat-free milk. Try getting at least three servings in every day. I read so many Internet "experts" write about swearing off dairy products, but that's not a good choice. The only dairy products I recommend you stay away from are whole fat-filled ones.

- ➤ Dairy contains calcium, which helps promote bone mass and healthy teeth. Three servings of milk daily will provide you with enough calcium.

- ➤ Certain dairy products, like yogurt and soymilk, provide potassium.

- ➤ Vitamin D is another nutrient with amazing benefit to the body as it also helps with bone development. Milk is a great source of Vitamin D.

- ➤ Skim milk produces endorphins in the brain in much the same way as soda, but it also provides important nutrients. You might still get the calories, but at least those calories are not wasted.

- ➤ Dairy products have been linked to a reduction in the risk of cardiovascular disease.

Certain dairy products have high levels of saturated fat, which will actually have a negative impact on your health. That's why this book tells you to choose from the low-fat/fat-free choices.

Chapter 2
DASH Dieting for Weight Loss

Even though this dieting plan was created for the sole purpose of lowering blood pressure and getting a handle on cholesterol, we're going to adapt it in a way that also makes it a powerful weight-loss tool. This dieting plan already puts an emphasis on eating food that is low in cholesterol and saturated fat. The fact that it will have you eating more whole foods will lead to a certain amount of weight-loss automatically.

What we're going to do is take the DASH diet and make a few minor tweaks to make it more efficient for losing weight.

Keep a Food Journal

Having a food journal gives you an easy way to go back to review your food consumption periodically. Write down every meal you eat and place a timestamp on it. This includes snacks and drinks—everything you put into your body should be documented. Take it a step further and document your activity while eating. For example, *"I had popcorn while watching a movie."*

It's easy to lose track of your food consumption, so documenting it gives you an easy way to go back and review it on a weekly basis. You can see where you stand in terms of your eating habits, so you can start fixing the bad ones.

Calculate Your Calorie Goal

If you are planning to lose weight, then you will have to lower your calorie intake, so that it's the same as what you burn on

a daily basis. But you must do it gradually so that it doesn't throw your metabolism out of whack.

Start out by determining exactly what activities you perform on a daily basis. Visit the following website for an amazing calculator:

https://www.healthstatus.com/calculate/cbc

When you determine how many calories you are burning per day, then you need to develop a plan. Here's an example:

You are burning 1,200 calories per day, so you will set up a list of goals as follows:

Week 1: 2,000 calories per day.

Week 2: 1,600 calories per day.

Week 3: 1,200 calories per day.

Make the Transition Slowly

When you make too many changes all at once, you will destabilize your body. This makes you crave your old diet, leading to relapses. It's extremely difficult to fight off your body's survival instincts, and that's exactly what your body does when it's in shock. It believes that survival is at risk, so it creates irresistible urges.

That's why it's important to make the transition slowly. Pace yourself by adapting to your new dietary plan so that your body doesn't even notice. You will eventually experience a

full change and wonder how you ever led an unhealthy lifestyle.

Reduce Your Consumption of Fat and Sugar Even Further

Even though the DASH diet is going to have you reducing trans and saturated fat intake, in order to lose weight you will need to avoid all types of fat in the beginning. Once you have reached your weight goal, then you can gradually work your way back up to the normal fats.

Stick to poultry and fish as your primary sources of meat. You should probably limit meat to once every day at most. Replace it with vegetables that are high in protein.

You will also need to reduce the sugars that you consume, including fruits in the beginning, if you want to lose weight. You should limit fruit consumption to one serving per day. Take a multi-vitamin to make up for the loss of nutrients. Once you have reached your weight loss goal, you can start to enjoy fruits as normal again.

Limit Sodium to 1,500 mg per Day

Remember when I said there were two types of DASH diet plans? You are going to want to opt for the one with less sodium intake. This is an area where so many people mess up when losing weight. They do everything right, except keeping their sodium intake down. Then they don't lose weight because the sodium causes their body to retain more water.

The main way to lower your sodium is by avoiding meats that are high in sodium. You will need to pay close attention to labels.

Eat More Vegetables and Whole Grains

Weight loss requires a few additional steps, one of which is to eat even more vegetables. Since you will need to reduce meat and sugar consumption in the initial stages, you will have to replace them with vegetables and whole grains. When I say whole grains, I mean everything–rice and noodles included.

Again, when using canned vegetables be sure that you read the label because some of those items are loaded with sodium and added sugar. Just keep in mind that you need to make these changes gradually to avoid shocking your system.

Fat-Free is Not Always Healthy

Fat-free does not always mean that a product is healthy. For example, some fat-free salad dressings contain even more calories than their fat-filled counterparts! That's why it's so important to read labels.

Most people will just blindly trust that the words "fat-free" mean healthier. That is definitely not always the case.

Distribute Your Calories Throughout the Day

Eating smaller portions of food throughout the entire day will help your body burn calories more efficiently because of the metabolic boost that accompanies it. If you are eating a super large dinner, then spread that meal throughout the

entire day. Usually, people who eat huge dinners skip lunch, which is a huge mistake.

Eating smaller portions is the absolute best habit you can develop for losing weight. Just this one change makes a huge difference. You should follow a specific meal pattern. The more consistent you are, the more efficient your body will function.

> ➢ Breakfast

> ➢ Morning snack

> ➢ Lunch

> ➢ Afternoon snack

> ➢ Dinner

> ➢ After-dinner snack (at least two hours before bed)

One of the final weight-loss tips for adding to the DASH diet is to exercise regularly, so the next chapter is dedicated to exercise.

Chapter 3
Exercise Plan

Now we're going to move onto a topic that drives so many people away from their weight-loss plans, but let me share a secret that you will not hear from other so-called experts:

You do not have to exercise to lose weight!

Exercise is optional, but it is highly recommended due to its many health benefits. But working out on its own is not enough to live a healthy lifestyle. Healthy eating is always the first and only required step. So I want you to look at exercise as an added bonus and not a requirement. That mindset will create realistic expectations on your part so that if you happen to miss a day of exercise, then you won't completely give up like so many others.

Weight-loss only requires you to create a calorie deficit, so you can choose any method you want as long as you are accomplishing that goal.

You cannot out-exercise a bad diet!

Consumption plays the biggest role in creating a calorie deficit. There are also other factors involved, including stress, sleep habits, and lifestyle choices. The truth is that the journey to a healthier lifestyle is a personal one that does not look the same for every person. What worked for those Internet "experts" might not work for you, and that's okay. So rather than allowing them to rip up your hopes and dreams, find your own path.

Keeping all of that in mind, exercise comes with a ton of benefits that will help you live a more productive life. So now that we understand that exercise shouldn't be placed on some unrealistic pedestal, let's dive deeper into the subject.

- Food choices are more important than workout choices.

- Exercise should become a meaningful part of your routine.

- If you exercise, you have to push yourself.

- You must find exercises that you enjoy; otherwise, you will skip them.

So you have the right expectations now, and we have set a lot of Internet opinions straight, so let's look at some actual workouts that you can do. While we're focusing on exercises that burn the most calories in the shortest amount of time, you are free to find other options if they fit your lifestyle better.

Interval Training

Interval training is the absolute best training method for getting into top shape. This form of exercise is designed to spike your heart rate and then allow it to come down multiple times during the same workout. An example of interval training will look something like this:

Goal: 10-Minute Walk

- Walk for 90 seconds.

- ➤ Run as fast as you can for 30 seconds.

- ➤ Walk for 90 seconds.

- ➤ Run as fast as you can for 30 seconds.

- ➤ Walk for 90 seconds.

- ➤ Run as fast as you can for 30 seconds.

- ➤ Walk for 90 seconds.

- ➤ Run as fast as you can for 30 seconds.

- ➤ Walk for 90 seconds.

- ➤ Run as fast as you can for 30 seconds.

Basically, you are going all-in for a short period of time and following it with an active rest. You can use this method for all of your exercise routines. Although it's not required, it will boost the efficiency of any workout. It's easily translated into indoor cycling, treadmill workouts, and weight training.

Weight Training is the King of All Weight-Loss Workouts

There is no better workout for weight-loss than resistance training, whether you're using weights or bands. Building muscle mass is the fastest way to lower fat volume. Weight training even boosts your idle metabolic rate, which means you continue to burn calories for hours after the workout. Additionally, the higher your muscle mass, the more calories you burn throughout the day. You can also go for longer with every workout, so you'll burn even more calories. Weight

training has a snowball effect in that its calorie burning potential increases exponentially as you build more muscle mass.

If this sounds like a path you want to explore, consider combining weight training with interval training. Then try creating a schedule that includes at least three sessions per week. Remember that if you miss a workout, then it's not the end of the world, so never give up.

Running

Cardio workouts are also a great choice for adding to your new lifestyle and weight-loss efforts. However, you cannot get lackadaisical here if you want to lose weight. That won't cut it. You need to include interval training here and pump up that heart rate! Better yet, set up that incline on your treadmill. Running uphill forces you to work your legs even more, leading to increased metabolism.

Running workouts are best done in the morning. While this rule is not set in stone, cardio workouts create an oxygen deficit in your body which means that it will have to work throughout the day to make up for the loss. As a result, your metabolic rate will be a significant boost.

If running is not your cup of tea, then you can try swimming instead. Of course, you will need access to a pool, so it's not exactly the most convenient form of exercise, but it is actually more efficient that running. Maybe mix up your cardio workouts by adding the occasional swimming routine?

Train Like a Boxer

At its core, boxing is just a form of interval training, but hitting a punching bag is an amazing form of stress relief. Just make sure you do it right. Beginners often use their arm strength to throw punches, but that's a mistake. The majority of punches should come from the core, using muscles that almost every other workout ignores.

Boxers often incorporate trainers to help them keep their intensity up, but you can find a few smartphone apps to help. Just make sure that you look up proper techniques so that you are getting the most from the exercise.

Jumping Rope

Kick it back to those old P.E. days, and break out the jump rope for an amazingly effective cardio workout. This is a cheap and portable tool, but more importantly, it's a lot of fun. It only takes a few minutes to get your heart racing. You probably won't want to jump rope every day, but you can use it periodically to add enjoyment to your workouts. Here's a quick and easy routine:

1. Do light rope skips for a minute to warm up.

2. Do 50 traditional jumps.

3. Follow up with 10 sprint jumps running as fast as you can.

4. Repeat Step 2 and Step 3 for 10 minutes.

Again, it's important to remember that exercise is not set in stone. The only thing that's necessary for the DASH diet is to eat healthy, so don't put exercise on such a high pedestal

that it becomes intimidating. Exercise is a powerful supporting mechanic of the DASH, diet but it's not the primary tool.

Chapter 4
Creating a Meal Plan

One of the first things that individuals ask when looking at any dieting plan is, "What foods are allowed?"

One of the best things about the DASH diet is that it doesn't have a ton of restrictions. Most foods can be eaten, and there is room for mistakes. Most fad diets are dependent on strict food choices, and even a slight deviation can throw them off balance. But the DASH diet is not like that. It's not some fad dieting plan. It's based around eating more fruits and vegetables while avoiding foods high in sodium.

- You might opt to eat a salad rather than a fast food burger and fries for lunch.

- You choose low-fat Greek yogurt instead of sweetened yogurt.

- You replace your afternoon snack cake with fruit.

Those are just three possible examples. Whole grains are also encouraged as part of a healthier lifestyle. Brown rice, whole wheat bread, and whole grain noodles are three examples.

With that said, you will have to avoid the following foods when following the DASH diet. Pretty much all food and drink that contains artificial sugar and is processed should be avoided. Again, we're just opting for natural over artificial.

- ➢ Candy

- Cookies

- Chips

- Salted nuts

- Sodas

- Sugary beverages

- Pastries

- Snack Foods like chips

- Prepackaged pasta and rice dishes (excluding macaroni and cheese because it is a separate category)

- Pizza

- Salad dressings

- Certain Cheeses

Salt is the most difficult because our taste buds are used to being overloaded with it. However, you can slowly lessen the amount of salt you put on food, and you'll never even notice.

There is also a substitute for salt that can be used that is potassium-based. Plus, it has the added benefit of lowering your blood pressure.

Red Meats and the DASH Diet

Eating too much red meat has been linked to increased heart disease. But honestly, as long as you don't consume red meat every day, then it's not going to be a problem. You're

going to be limiting meats to just two servings per day anyway.

If you want to enhance the DASH diet even further, then you can choose grass-fed beef because it falls under a different category than traditional grain-fed beef. Grass-red beef is loaded with omega-3s and is actually similar to fish as far as nutrition is concerned. Grain-fed beef is loaded with saturated fat, which contributes to heart disease.

Again, I am not going to put any one rule on a pedestal. Avoid traditional red meats when possible, but you don't have to avoid them altogether. There are some amazingly healthy recipes that call for beef. But try to keep it as lean as possible or opt for grass-fed.

An Average Day Following the DASH Diet

Let's take a look at the typical day when following the DASH diet. You will also find a full four-week meal plan and recipes at the end of this book. For now, I want you to know what you should expect.

A typical day will look something like this:

> ➢ 2 servings of lean meat or protein-based plant

> ➢ 2 cups of vegetables

> ➢ 2 servings of fruit

> ➢ 2 servings fat-free dairy products

> ➢ 2-4 servings of whole grain

> ➢ 2 tsp. olive oil (or other healthy oil)

> ➤ 1 oz. nuts or seeds

Here's a quick look at a sample menu:

Breakfast: Oatmeal with pecans, ½ apple, and cinnamon.

Morning Snack: ½ apple and 1 tsp. peanut butter.

Lunch: Green salad with other mixed vegetables, grilled skinless, boneless chicken breast, and vinaigrette. The trick to salads is to dip your fork into the dressing before using it to grab the salad for a bite. That way, you do not saturate your salad with dressing.

Afternoon snack: Carrot sticks or a palm-full of nuts.

Dinner: Ground-turkey zucchini pasta with marinara.

Dessert: 1 serving of Greek yogurt with strawberries.

Create Your Own Personalized Meal Plan

Now that we have looked through some of the food requirements, I'm going to show you the three steps to creating your very own personalized meal plan.

Step 1: Have a List of Foods That Are Allowed with Each Meal
Let's keep things as simple as possible, so break down each meal into simple. You should create a chart so you can look at it when making your meal plan. I also recommend you plan out your meals a week in advance. Doing this helps keep you on track. Making meal decisions when you're hungry is never a good idea.

Your meal plans will look something like this:

Breakfast: 1 whole grain + 1 fruit/nut

Snack: 1 fruit/nut (opposite of breakfast)

Lunch: 1 vegetable + 1 leafy green + 1 protein

Snack: 1 vegetable of 1 fruit

Dinner: 1 protein + 1 whole grain + 1 vegetable

Dessert: 1 fruit + 1 fat-free dairy product

Breakfast: 1 protein +1 fruit (+ vegetables if desired)

Step 2: Portion Your Food

Once you have a basic breakdown of how you want to plan each meal, you will need to get familiar with portioning. Each food group has a different way to portion food. Portioning is one of the most important factors in pretty much any dieting plan. You have to keep track of what you put into your body. Each of the following is considered one portion:

Protein

- ➢ 3 oz. poultry or lean beef when fully cooked

- ➢ 4 oz. fish or shellfish when fully cooked

- ➢ 5 oz. tofu

Dairy

- ➢ ½ cup milk

- ➢ 1 cup yogurt

- ➢ 1 whole egg

29

Fruit

> ➢ 1 cup berries or cut-up fruit

> ➢ 1 whole fruit

> ➢ 1 palm full of fried fruit

> ➢ ½ cup fruit juice (no sugar added)

Vegetables

> ➢ 1 cup of any vegetable

Whole Grains

> ➢ ½ cup brown rice, pasta, etc.

> ➢ 1 slice whole grain bread

> ➢ ½ sweet potato with no additives

> ➢ 2 medium tortillas, whole-grain

It's important to note that this list is not necessarily set in stone, nor will it follow the labels of certain products. Make sure you read the serving size on a label when adding up its numbers. Don't base label number off of this list.

Step 3: Create Menus
Now that you have a better understanding of portion sizes, it's time to actually put your meals together. I recommend you create a template so that you can just fill it out from week to week, then plug in the actual dishes. Again, the end of this book is going to include a four-week meal plan to help you get started.

You will want to print this menu out and post it somewhere you can see it every day.

Chapter 5
Out with the Old, In with the New

All lifestyle changes come down to willpower, but did you know that willpower is not based on strength or resolve? It's based on making smart changes. You see, we're only human, so when we are faced with too much temptation, we will fall victim to it. It's only a matter of time. People who have a lot of willpower make smart choices to remove the temptation from their life.

Therefore, if your goal is to live a healthier life, then you will need to get all of that junk food out of your pantry. That's the only way you'll ever be able to completely give it up. Cravings happen, and the biological urge to snack will become too great to ignore. But if the food is not accessible, then the temptation will be much lower.

This chapter is going to show you exactly what you should be targeting when you start looking for organizing your pantry to accommodate your new lifestyle.

Be warned that this is a difficult step, so you will have to be courageous!

It's Time to Make Some Difficult Choices
As with any new lifestyle, you will have some difficult choices to make, so it's time to summon up your courage and make them right now. If you're reading this book, then you are looking to live a healthier lifestyle. You will need to remove temptation.

Most people have a pantry full of food that's just awful for their health. Did you know that the majority of people who try a new dieting plan do not get rid of the unhealthy food from their home? They make up all kinds of excuses, but the bottom line is that this is a step you absolutely must take. If you are married or in a committed relationship, then your partner will have to be on-board with this new lifestyle. If they truly care about your health, then they'll understand that this is a step that you must take.

Throw Away (or Donate) All Unhealthy Food

These foods will continue to hold your health hostage until you remove them from your life. You are essentially creating a clean slate for your health. Get a large trash can, drag it into your kitchen, and start going through your pantry, throwing away any food that does not meet the DASH dieting requirements. You can also donate non-perishable food to your local community pantry, church, or soup kitchen. Here is your plan of attack!

Phase 1: Throw out All Obvious Junk
This includes candy, soda, chips, and everything else that you know is unhealthy. You're going to go shopping right after you finish here so don't worry if your pantry gets bare. You are wiping the slate clean. We are going to be replacing your unhealthy snacks with healthy ones. All obvious junk food should be gone by the end of this phase.

Phase 2: Use the Nutrition Label to Decide What Goes Next
As I mentioned earlier in the book, you will need to get accustomed to reading labels if you want to start leading a healthier life. We're going to use that knowledge now to get

rid of some of those unhealthy items from your kitchen. Here is a step-by-step look:

1. Read the List of Ingredients: Ingredients on a label are listed in descending order, starting with the highest concentration. In layman's terms, an ingredient that the product contains the most of will be listed first. If you see any sugars, fats, oils, and salts listed first, then you can assume that the food will not be a healthy option.

2. Look at the Nutritional Facts: Does the food contain any valuable vitamins and/or minerals?

3. Look at the Serving Size: You will want to pay attention to the size of each serving. Some brands will place smaller servings so that their nutritional information appears to be healthier.

4. Calories per Serving: Compare the serving size to how many calories are in it. If a small serving size is accompanied by a lot of calories, then chances are that the food is unhealthy. In general:

> 40 or less calories per serving is low

> 100 calories per serving is moderate

> 400 calories per serving is considered high and should always be avoided

5. Fat and Sodium: You will need to limit your sodium intake to at least 2,100 mg. per day (1,600 for weight-loss). Furthermore, avoid saturated and trans fats. You should

consume no more than 16 grams and 2 grams respectively. Foods that are super high in these fats are junk.

6. Vitamins and Fiber: You must consume 100% of the daily value of all nutrients.

7. Daily Value Percentage: This tells you the percentage of a specific nutrient you get in a single serving. Five percent or less is the best for saturated fats, cholesterol, and sodium. Anything more should be avoided.

You will be able to get rid of some more junk food by just glancing at the label. If you're not sure, place it to the side for the next step.

Phase 3: Decide on Difficult Items

Some of the items are going to be difficult to decide on. If you're unsure of a product, then just go ahead and get rid of it. You'll know what foods are good for you and which ones are not. Snacks and chips are an easy choice, but it gets more difficult when you find those canned soups and frozen pizzas that you depend on for a quick snack. If you want to lead a healthier life, you need to get rid of them. Create your own healthy quick snacks.

Look, I can't be there with you, so the choice is ultimately yours to make. But I will promise you that if you keep unhealthy foods around, then you're going to eventually fall prey to the temptation they represent. Willpower can never be greater than biology, and your biological cravings will always eventually win.

We're Out With the Old, Now it's Time to Bring In the New

At this point, your cabinets, fridge, and freezer are all bare. So it's time to refill them with healthier choices. But you will need to plan ahead before you step foot into a grocery store. There are two golden rules when grocery shopping that you must follow:

Golden Rule 1: Always make a shopping list, and never deviate from it. If you see something you want that is not on the list, write it down and put it on your next shopping list. Never, ever buy food that is not on your list!

Golden Rule 2: Always shop right after a meal. Never go grocery shopping when you're hungry. When you shop hungry, you are going to be tempted to deviate from your list and make unhealthy choices.

Some of your favorite foods can be substituted for something that's healthier without making much of a sacrifice. For example, if you love chips, then you're much more likely to follow through if you change over to popcorn rather than swapping over to dried fruit. My point is that it's okay to take small steps here.

> ➤ Instead of chips, try air-popped popcorn. Eventually, you can add in dried fruit as a snack.

> ➤ Instead of frozen burritos, try homemade burritos made with healthy ingredients.

> ➤ If you must have bacon, then try turkey bacon. Just be sure to eat low sodium.

➢ If you love beef jerky, try turkey jerky instead. Better yet, make your own!

➢ You can eat mixed nuts in moderation as long as they are unsalted.

➢ Tortilla chips and salsa are a healthier alternative (in moderation) to Cheetos or other unhealthy chips. You can even try apple or banana chips!

➢ Hummus and guacamole are great alternatives to dipping sauces.

➢ Greek yogurt sweetened with fruit is a great sweet-tooth treat to replace those Little Debbie cakes.

➢ Dark chocolate is perfectly okay as long as it's eaten in moderation.

➢ Freeze sliced bananas and then process them using a food processor to make healthy, and delicious banana ice cream. You can do the same with seedless grapes.

➢ Sour foods can be substituted with citrus like oranges, kiwi, and even grapefruit.

➢ Low-fat cheeses can be used to make certain cheesy dishes.

Make sure you include a lot of whole grains on your list. This includes bread, pasta, and rice. Stay away from white flour foods.

Those are just examples, but you can use your label reading abilities in combination with common sense to replace favorites slowly. Keep in mind that right now, your taste buds have been programmed to like foods that are actually not that great. You're just so used to them that they have become routine, and the body does not like change. Your taste buds are replaced every two weeks, so that's all it takes to grow accustomed to lower sodium and healthier foods.

If you eat whole foods for just two weeks without cheating, you will start to realize that those foods you used to love are actually not that great.

The goal here is to find healthier alternatives to foods that you really enjoy. Be sure that you read the label before putting an item into your shopping cart.

Final Tips Before Heading to the Grocery Store

I'm sure you're ready to make that first trip to the grocery store, so let's go over a few more tips that you need to follow beforehand.

Don't get obsessed with the small things. Be smart and use your best judgment. If you make a mistake, it's not the end of the world. Just follow your list to the letter, and learn from any mistakes you make. Again, never deviate from your list.

Moderation is essential to healthier living. Some of your favorite foods are not going to have super healthy alternatives. That's okay! Just find an alternative that's healthier and then enjoy it in moderation. You're not going to

follow any lifestyle for the long-term if you give up everything you enjoy.

Utilize technology to help. There are a lot of powerful tools out there that can help you manage your shopping lists and food menus. One of the best tools is Evernote, since you can access it from multiple devices. Tools like Calorie Counter will also help you track your daily calorie consumption, though I recommend you start out by using a pen and paper since it's a more personal approach.

Create your own cookbook. When you come across a recipe that you love, print it out, and place it into a binder so that you have easy access to it later. It will help motivate you to continue your journey. Eventually, you will have a thick binder full of healthy recipes.

Chapter 6
DASH Dieting Tips for Long--Term Success

The most important mindset that you will ever develop in life is to always find ways to challenge and improve yourself. There is always room for self-improvement. The moment you stop improving yourself is the moment you accept failure.

Challenge yourself to take an action to improve yourself every day!

This is true for all aspects of your life, whether it's your health or career. You absolutely must always take action to improve every day if you want to continue to find success.

Find Personal Motivation

Personal motivation will help keep you excited about meeting your goals so that it's easier to meet your health goals. For example, if you are concerned about the environment but don't want to necessarily give up meat, then look for ways of purchasing meat that is raised in a way that's environmentally friendly. Grass-fed beef is more sustainable than corn-fed. Free-range chicken is more environmentally friendly than farm-raised.

My point is that when you attach a personal motivation to your dieting plan, then you'll be far more likely to follow through. The problem that so many of us have when starting a new dieting plan is that we have been on this rollercoaster ride for so long that we don't know any different. Past failures

from impossible plans have caused us to lose most of our motivation, so we go into it half-hearted.

Answer these four questions to find your personal motivation:

> ➢ How many different dieting plans have you tried in the past?

> ➢ What caused you to fail them?

> ➢ What is different now that will help lead you to success?

> ➢ Why are you trying to make this change?

Use something personal as motivation. If your family has a history of heart disease, then the fact that you need to lower your risk of heart disease by eating healthier can be a powerful motivator. It's okay to be selfish here. The only thing that matters is that it serves as a personal motivation so that it helps you stick to your goals.

Stick to Your Goals

By this point, you have reequipped your kitchen with healthy food options and gotten rid of everything that's unhealthy. Now is when the real challenge begins. You have to make sure that it doesn't fall apart when you make a mistake–and you will make a mistake. It's going to happen, so you need to accept that now. And you know what? Making mistakes is okay as long as you learn from them and don't keep repeating the same mistake over and over again.

A short session with a nutritionist can help you get started, but feel free to watch some YouTube videos if you don't have

access to a personal nutritionist. A professional can help you adapt this new lifestyle into your personal life according to your own preferences. Plus, they serve as a support network.

Another important piece of advice (and this goes for any major life change) is that you absolutely must have a network of friends who support your decisions. If your friends mock or poke fun of your new healthy lifestyle, then you will need to find a new group to spend most of your time with. I know that a lot of you are going to pass over this advice, but your network of friends will influence you. An individual is the sum of the five people they are around the most, so if those people are mocking your choices then you'll eventually start to believe those negative connotations.

I am not saying that you have to cut them out of your life, but you benefit from limiting your exposure to those people. Develop a network of like-minded people who share your goals.

How to Keep Others from Undermining Your Choices

Ever had a co-worker bring in a plate of homemade muffins when you're trying to lose weight? When you refuse them, everyone gives you the cold shoulder or tries to convince you that "just one won't hurt."

Developing new habits is difficult enough, so it's not helpful when that commitment is met with resistance from other people. Most people do one of two things: they get defensive and reply with a snarky comment, leading to resentment, or they cave to peer-pressure.

It's essential that you understand these critiques are not meant to be malicious. They are simply the result of people who have fallen victim to misinformation, either believing some Internet myth they've read somewhere or disappointed in their own health-related decisions.

Always have an open mind. Listen to what they have to say, and then decide whether it's relevant to your situation. If you believe that your decision is sound, then stick to your guns. Here are a few common scenarios that you will likely encounter, and productive ways to fend off the flak.

Thanksgiving Dinner

Family is tricky. They do care about you, but they also have their own personal views. In most cases, their viewpoints are set in stone. They might know that you have a new healthy-eating lifestyle, but they still pass you those unhealthy foods on Thanksgiving:

"Just eat it. It won't kill you!"

"It's just one day. It won't mess up your diet."

"But it's your favorite, and I made it just for you!"

The last one is a bit ironic because if they made it just for you, and you're trying to live a cleaner, healthier life, then they actually did not make it just for you.

What to Do

Dealing with family is tricky because you don't want to be disrespectful. But you cannot give in to their lack of commitment. Most older people are from the generation

where you express love through food. We're trying to detach emotion from food, an action that they simply don't understand. You cannot break through that strong belief.

The best way to deal with this situation is to just smile and continue eating what you had originally planned. Then if they keep insisting, say that you're full and ask to take some home with you instead. Once you get the food to your home, you can do whatever you want with it.

If they push too hard, then remember that it's your life, and you do not have to go to their Thanksgiving dinner.

The Barbeque

A scenario that is quite common for vegetarians is going to a friend's barbeque. While your friend might be completely supportive of your lifestyle and even grill you a veggie burger, others at the event might be less supportive. Vegetarians hear these things quite often:

"How can you live without bacon?"

"How can you eat that? It's gross!"

"Humans were meant to eat meat!"

"You aren't getting enough protein!"

These are all such untrue statements, so it can get frustrating. Always remember that it's your choice what you put into your body, so if you do not want to eat meat, then what these people say really doesn't matter. Pressure comes from people telling us what they think we should do, so it's easy to forget that we're ultimately in control of ourselves.

What to Do

You deal with this situation by being positive. "My burger is delicious! You should try it before you knock it."

Negative people don't respond to confidence, so they will leave you alone either way.

Visiting Your Hometown

Seeing your hometown friends and family might be nostalgic, but it comes at the cost of receiving a ton of unsolicited advice and commentary about your life. You'll hear things like:

"You must exercise all of the time!"

"Are you eating enough because you look too thin?"

"You could stand to eat a cheeseburger!"

That last comment is the one that gets me the most. People are judgmental of your health choices when it threatens them. Jealously leads to negative criticism, but rather than letting it bother you, just move on.

What to Do

"There is no need to worry about my health. My doctor says that I am healthy."

"I have never felt better in my life!"

Those are two generic responses that you can use to respond to those people. I don't recommend you shift it back on them because they will only get more defensive. It's

human nature to lash out when we feel threatened, but avoid that trait. Kindness always wins.

The Dinner Party

Most foods at these parties are a disaster for your health. You try your best to lightly fill your plate, but everyone seems to notice.

"You're barely even eating."

"Don't you like real food?"

The fact that you shouldn't have to explain what you eat to others doesn't seem to matter because everyone stares and wants an explanation.

What to Do

First of all, don't let anyone pressure you into making unhealthy choices. You can also redirect the conversation to get them chatting about something else. They real key is to be polite and not let it get to you.

"I don't want to try everything at once. I am pacing myself. By the way, how was your vacation?"

Office Lunch

Everyone decides to grab lunch from a local fast-food chain so you politely decline. Yet, someone brings you back a large order of fries or a burger anyway.

"You can afford to be unhealthy for one meal."

"It's not that bad for you!"

"You need to live a little."

This is actually the same type of peer pressure that drug dealers use to get their clients hooked. People have a tough time saying no to free stuff because it's considered "impolite."

What to Do

You are allowed to pass on food that you're offered, even if someone bought it. You never asked for it, so saying no is not impolite. Just remember to keep it civilized.

"Thanks for the offer, but I brought my own lunch."

"Thanks, but I don't like fast food. I prefer to eat my lunch."

When Your Workout Buddy Bails

You have scheduled regular workouts with your friend, but she bails for the third day in a row.

"Let's just do it tomorrow. Netflix sure beats hitting the grindstone!"

"Wouldn't you rather take a break?"

"What's the big deal?"

The big deal is that your friend made a commitment, so it can be frustrating when they use the same excuses over and over. With that said, there's no reason to blacklist them.

What to Do

You can acknowledge that rest days are an important part of an exercise plan, but make sure you stick to your plan of action. You can start off with a friendly response like:

"That does sounds awesome, but I really have to get this workout in today. We can meet up this weekend, though, if you want."

If the pattern continues, you might need to find a new workout buddy.

Final Thoughts

The DASH diet was developed to lower blood pressure, but it was modified it in a way to work as an efficient weight-loss tool. Unlike other fad diets scattered around the Internet, this one is backed by numerous studies and has been ranked #1 by *U.S. News & World Report*. It effectively reduces the risk of certain cancers, heart disease, kidney stones, and diabetes. Though what should motivate you the most is that it's loaded with amazing food choices, so it's the most sustainable dieting plan in the world.

The following sections of this book will give you a four-week meal plan that you can follow to help you get started. You will also find several amazing recipes that incorporate foods that are 100 percent compatible with the DASH diet. As you'll quickly learn, most of these food choices are tastier than all of those processed foods that most people stuff their faces with.

DASH dieting is recommended by:

➢ The National Heart, Lung, and Blood Institute

➢ The American Heart Association

➢ The Dietary Guidelines for Americans

Remember that it's your life, so no matter what anyone says, what you put into your body is your choice.

Four-Week
Meal Plan

Meal Plan Introduction

The following section is going to outline a four-week meal plan to help you get started. There are a few things to keep in mind before you follow through with any meal plan though.

1. You are allowed to mix and match this meal plan however you want. Don't be afraid to experiment.

2. Some of these meals include leftovers since certain recipes will make more than one meal. That's okay because it gives you a break from having to cook every night.

3. Lunches can be made the night before so that you can just grab it on your way out the door.

4. Learning to limit your portion size is essential. It's going to seem difficult at first because you're probably used to overeating. But over time, it gets much easier.

Week 1

Monday

Breakfast: Hard-boiled egg, bacon, and juice

Morning Snack: Palm-full of nuts

Lunch: Tuna salad sandwich with lettuce

Afternoon Snack: 1 Apple

Dinner: Quinoa meatless alls

Dessert: Fig and honey yogurt

Tuesday

Breakfast: Buckwheat pancakes

Snack: ½ Banana

Lunch: Tuna salad sandwich with lettuce (leftover from Monday)

Snack: ½ Banana

Dinner: Lemon-garlic shrimp over orzo with zucchini

Dessert: Yogurt with nuts and raspberries

Wednesday

Breakfast: Hard-boiled egg, bacon, and juice

Snack: ½ Apple and palm-full of nuts

Lunch: Quinoa meatless balls (Leftover from Monday)

Snack: ½ Apple

Dinner: Lemon-garlic shrimp over orzo with zucchini (leftover from Tuesday)

Dessert: Grape ice cream (frozen grapes put through food processor)

Thursday

Breakfast: 1 Piece of whole grain toast and 1 orange

Snack: ½ Banana and palm-full of nuts

Lunch: Green salad with Ppita bread and hummus

Snack: ½ Banana and palm-full of nuts

Dinner: Chicken chili with sweet potatoes with avocado and yogurt

Dessert: Included in dinner

Friday

Breakfast: Peanut-butter cinnamon toast

Snack: ½ Grapefruit

Lunch: Chicken chili with sweet potatoes (leftover from Thursday)

Snack: ½ Grapefruit

Dinner: Asian pork tenderloin

Dessert: Banana ice cream (frozen bananas put through food processor)

Saturday

Breakfast: Hard-boiled egg, bacon, and juice

Snack: ½ banana and palm-full of nuts

Lunch: Asian pork tenderloin (leftover from Friday)

Snack: ½ Banana and palm-full of nuts

Dinner: Mediterranean-style chicken kabobs

Dessert: Yogurt with nuts and raspberries

Sunday

Breakfast: Mini-egg beaters southwestern style omelet

Snack: 1 Apple

Lunch: Turkey and pear pita melt

Snack: Palm full of nuts

Dinner: Curried cauliflower steaks with red rice

Dessert: Fig and honey yogurt

Week 2

Monday

Breakfast: Hard-boiled egg, bacon, and juice

Snack: ½ Banana and palm-full of nuts

Lunch: Green salad with pita bread and hummus

Snack: ½ Banana and palm-full of nuts

Dinner: Broccoli, garlic, and rigatoni

Dessert: Yogurt with nuts and raspberries

Tuesday

Breakfast: Buckwheat pancakes

Snack: ½ Banana

Lunch: Broccoli, garlic, and rigatoni (leftover from Monday)

Snack: ½ Banana

Dinner: Curried cauliflower steaks with red rice

Dessert: Yogurt with nuts and raspberries

Wednesday

Breakfast: Mini-egg beaters southwestern style omelet

Snack: 1 Apple

Lunch: Buffalo chicken salad wrap

Snack: Palm full of nuts

Dinner: Grilled Asian salmon

Dessert: Fig and honey yogurt

Thursday

Breakfast: Egg with salsa and toast

Snack: ½ Banana and palm-full of nuts

Lunch: Curried cauliflower steaks with red rice (leftover from Tuesday)

Snack: ½ Banana and palm-full of nuts

Dinner: Beef stew with fennel and shallots

Dessert: Included in dinner

Friday

Breakfast: Mini-egg beaters southwestern style omelet

Snack: 1 Apple

Lunch: Buffalo chicken salad wrap

Snack: Palm-full of nuts

Dinner: Beef stew with fennel and shallots (leftover from Thursday)

Dessert: Grape ice cream (frozen grapes put through food processor)

Saturday

Breakfast: Buckwheat pancakes

Snack: ½ Banana

Lunch: Mediterranean chicken with orzo salad

Snack: ½ Banana

Dinner: Mediterranean chicken with orzo salad (leftover from Lunch)

Dessert: Yogurt with nuts and raspberries

Sunday

Breakfast: Peanut-butter cinnamon toast

Snack: ½ Grapefruit

Lunch: Turkey and pear pita melt

Snack: ½ Grapefruit

Dinner: Quinoa meatless balls

Dessert: Banana ice cream (frozen bananas put through food processor)

Week 3

Monday

Breakfast: Mini-egg beaters southwestern style omelet

Snack: 1 Apple

Lunch: Quinoa meatless balls (leftover from Sunday)

Snack: Palm-full of nuts

Dinner: Lemon-herb salmon with caponata and farro

Dessert: Fig and honey yogurt

Tuesday

Breakfast: Peanut-butter cinnamon toast

Snack: ½ Grapefruit

Lunch: Lemon-herb salmon with caponata and farro (leftover from Monday)

Snack: ½ Grapefruit

Dinner: Stuffed sweet potato with hummus dressing

Dessert: Banana ice cream (frozen bananas put through food processor)

Wednesday

Breakfast: Egg with salsa and toast

Snack: ½ Banana and palm-full of nuts

Lunch: Stuffed sweet potato with hummus dressing (leftover from Tuesday)

Snack: ½ Banana ad palm-full of nuts

Dinner: Beef stew with fennel and shallots

Dessert: Fig and honey yogurt

Thursday

Breakfast: Hard-boiled egg, bacon, and uice

Snack: ½ Banana and palm-full of nuts

Lunch: Salmon pita sandwich

Snack: ½ Banana and palm-full of nuts

Dinner: Beef stew with fennel and shallots (leftover from Wednesday)

Dessert: Yogurt with nuts and raspberries

Friday

Breakfast: Buckwheat pancakes

Snack: ½ Banana

Lunch: Tuna salad sandwich

Snack: ½ Banana

Dinner: Mediterranean chicken with orzo salad

Dessert: Yogurt with nuts and raspberries

Saturday

Breakfast: 1 Piece of whole grain toast and 1 orange

Snack: ½ Banana and palm full of nuts

Lunch: Tuna salad sandwich

Snack: ½ Banana and palm-full of nuts

Dinner: Mediterranean chicken with orzo salad (leftover from Friday)

Dessert: Yogurt with nuts and raspberries

Sunday

Breakfast: Mini-egg beaters southwestern style omelet

Snack: 1 Apple

Lunch: Turkey and pear pita melt

Snack: Palm-full of nuts

Dinner: Curried cauliflower steaks with red rice

Dessert: Fig and honey yogurt

Week 4

Monday

Breakfast: Buckwheat pancakes

Snack: ½ Banana

Lunch: Curried cauliflower steaks with red rice (leftover from Sunday)

Snack: ½ Banana

Dinner: Mediterranean chicken with orzo salad

Dessert: Yogurt with nuts and raspberries

Tuesday

Breakfast: Hard-boiled egg, bacon, and juice

Morning Snack: Palm-full of nuts

Lunch: Veggie-hummus sandwich

Afternoon Snack: 1 Apple

Dinner: Quinoa meatless balls

Dessert: Fig and honey yogurt

Wednesday

Breakfast: Peanut-butter cinnamon toast

Snack: ½ Grapefruit

Lunch: Tuna salad sandwich

Snack: ½ Grapefruit

Dinner: Quinoa meatless balls (leftover from Wednesday)

Dessert: Banana ice cream (frozen bananas put through food processor)

Thursday

Breakfast: Egg with salsa and toast

Snack: ½ Banana and palm-full of nuts

Lunch: Tuna salad sandwich

Snack: ½ Banana and palm-full of nuts

Dinner: Chicken chili with sweet potatoes with avocado and yogurt

Dessert: Included in dinner

Friday

Breakfast: 1 Piece of whole grain toast + 1 orange

Snack: ½ Banana + palm-full of nuts

Lunch: Chicken chili with sweet potatoes with avocado and yogurt (leftover from Thursday)

Snack: ½ Banana and palm-full of nuts

Dinner: Creamy fettuccine with brussel sprouts and mushrooms

Dessert: Grape ice cream (frozen grapes put through food processor)

Saturday

Breakfast: Mini-egg beaters southwestern style omelet

Snack: 1 Apple

Lunch: Turkey and pear pita melt

Snack: Palm-full of nuts

Dinner: Gazpacho with chickpeas

Dessert: Fig and honey yogurt

Sunday

Breakfast: Buckwheat pancakes

Snack: ½ Banana

Lunch: White Bean and avocado salad

Snack: ½ Banana

Dinner: Mediterranean-style chicken kabobs

Dessert: Yogurt with nuts and raspberries

Recipes

Asian Pork Tenderloin

Servings: 2

o ½ Lb. pork tenderloin, sliced into approximately 4 Oz. portions

o 1 Tbsp. sesame seeds

o ½ Tsp. coriander, ground

o Dash of cayenne pepper

o Dash of celery seed

o ¼ Tsp. minced onion

o 1/8 Tsp. cumin, ground

o Dash of ground cinnamon

o ½ Tbsp. sesame oil

1. Preheat oven at 400 degrees. While waiting, coat a baking dish lightly with cooking spray.

2. Add a single layer of sesame seeds to a frying pan and cook at a low heat. Stir seeds until they are a golden color– usually 1 minute. Remove from pan.

3. Mix toasted sesame seeds, celery seed, coriander, cumin, cinnamon, cayenne pepper, minced onion, and sesame oil in a bowl.

4. Place pork tenderloins into a lightly sprayed baking dish. Rub mixture on both side of pork. Bake for 10-15 minutes until pork reaches 170 degrees in the center.

Macros (per serving)

Calories: 385

Fat: 20g.

Carbs: 16g.

Protein: 37g.

Beef Stew with Fennel and Shallots

Servings: 4

- 3 Tbsp. flour, all-purpose

- 1 Lb. boneless, cubed, lean beef stewing meat (trim away all fat possible)

- 2 Tbsp. olive oil

- ½ Trimmed, thinly sliced fennel bulb

- 3 Chopped shallots

- ¾ Tsp. black pepper

- 2 Thyme sprigs, fresh

- 1 Bay leaf

- 3 Cups vegetable broth, salt-free

- 4 Peeled and chunked carrots

- 4 Peeled and chunked potatoes, red or white skinned

- 18 Small onions for boiling, cut into halves

- 3 Portobello mushrooms, chunked and cleaned

- 1/3 Cup chopped parsley

1. Heat oil in a saucepan on medium. Coat beef cubes in flour and add to the oil, browning on all sides–approximately 5 minutes. Remove beef from pan.

2. Add shallots and fennel to the pan. Saute on medium for approximately 7 minutes until soft. Add ¼ Tsp. pepper, thyme sprigs, and bay leaf to the mix. Saute for an additional minute.

3. Place beef back into the pan with new mixture. Add in vegetable stock and cover. Simmer on low for 45 minutes.

4. Mix in carrots, potatoes, onions, and mushrooms. Note that the liquid will not completely cover the vegetables, but more liquid will form as the mushrooms cook. Simmer this new mixture for an additional 30 minutes.

5. Remove thyme sprigs and bay leaf, discarding them both. Stir in parsley and the remainder of pepper.

6. You can now serve.

Macros (per serving)

Calories: 440

Fat: 8.5g.

Carbs: 62g.

Protein: 27g

Broccoli, Garlic, and Rigatoni

Servings: 5

- o   3 Oz. whole-wheat rigatoni noodles

- o   1 Cup Broccoli florets

- o   1 Tbsp. parmesan cheese

- o   1 Tsp. olive oil

- o   1 Tsp. minced garlic

- o   Dash of ground, black pepper

1. Fill a large pot three-quarters full with water. Bring it to a boil. Add in pasts and cook for approximately 7-10 minutes, or until pasta is tender. Drain water from pasta.

2. Bring another pot of water (1 inch deep) with a steamer basket to a boil and add broccoli to the basket. Steam broccoli until tender, approximately 7 minutes.

3. Combine pasta and broccoli in a large bowl. Toss in Parmesan cheese, olive oil, and garlic.

Macros (per serving)

Calories: 608

Fat: 29g.

Carbs: 74g.

Protein: 16g

Buckwheat Pancakes

Servings: 4

- 1 Egg White

- ½ Tbsp. canola oil

- ¼ Cup skim milk

- ¼ Cup flour, all purpose

- ¼ Cup buckwheat flour

- ½ Tbsp. baking powder

- ½ Tbsp. sugar (optional)

- ¼ Cup sparkling water

- 1 ½ Cup strawberries, sliced

1. Whisk egg white, oil, and milk together in a bowl.

2. Mix together baking powder, flours, and sugar in another bowl. Then add in mixture from step 1 and water until the flour is moist.

3. Use a non-stick pan over middle heat to cook pancakes. Once the pan has been heated, place ½ cup of mixture and cook, flipping until golden brown. It takes approximately 3-4 minutes to cook each pancake.

4. Serve with strawberries, rather than syrup.

Macros (per serving)

Calories: 196

Fat: 6g.

Carbs: 26g.

Protein: 9g

Buffalo Chicken Salad Wrap

Servings: 4

- 3 Oz. Skinless, boneless chicken breasts
- 2 Chipotle peppers, whole
- ¼ Cup white wine vinegar
- ¼ Cup low-calorie mayonnaise
- 2 Stalks diced celery
- 2 Carrots, cut into matchstick-style lengths
- 1 Yellow onion, small
- ½ Rutabaga, sliced
- 4 Oz. Spinach, cut into strips
- 2 Tortillas, whole-grain

1. Preheat oven to 375 degrees. Then bake chicken for 10 minutes per side until inside temperature is 165 degrees.

2. Remove chicken and allow to cool. Then cut it into cubes.

3. Use a blender to dice and mix peppers with the vinegar and mayonnaise.

4. Place mixture, along with rutabaga, diced onion, chicken, and celery into a bowl. Mix thoroughly.

5. Place mixture and spinach evenly over both tortillas and wrap them. Cut in half to create 1 serving. Store the rest in a plastic bag for use later.

Macros (per serving)

Calories: 327

Fat: 11g.

Carbs: 28g.

Protein: 33g

Chicken Chili with Sweet Potatoes with Avocado and Yogurt

Servings: 6

- 2 Cups cooked chicken cut into ½ inch cubes

- 1 Cup frozen corn

- 2 Tbsp. extra-virgin olive oil

- 1 Chopped onion

- 3 Minced garlic cloves

- 2 Cups cubed sweet potatoes

- 1 Chopped green bell pepper

- 2 Tbsp. chili powder

- 2 Tsp. ground cumin

- 1 Tsp. oregano, dried

- 15 Oz. rinsed cannellini beans

- 2 Cups chicken broth

- ¾ Tsp. salt

- ¼ Tsp pepper

- ¼ Diced avocado

- 1 Tbsp. Greek yogurt, nonfat and plain

78

1. Heat olive oil in a pot on medium-high. Add onion, garlic, sweet potato, and bell pepper. Cook for 5 minutes, stirring occasionally. All vegetables must be slightly soft. Stir chili powder, oregano, and cumin into the mix. Cook an additional minute.

2. Add beans and broth to the mixture. Bring it all to a boil, reduce heat, and then gently simmer for an additional 15 minutes.

3. Increase heat again to medium-high. Stir in corn and cook for 1 additional minute.

4. Add chicken and cook for 2 more minutes.

5. Remove from heat, stir in salt and pepper. Top with avocado and yogurt.

Macros (per serving)

Calories: 277

Fat: 14g.

Carbs: 20g.

Protein: 17g

Creamy Fettuccine with Brussel Sprouts and Mushrooms

Servings: 6

- o 4 Cups brussel sprouts, sliced
- o 12 Oz. fettuccine, whole-wheat
- o 1 Tbsp. extra-virgin olive oil
- o 4 Cups mixed mushrooms, sliced.
- o 1 Tbsp. minced garlic
- o 2 Tbsp. sherry vinegar
- o 2 Cups low-fat milk
- o 2 Tbsp. flour, all-purpose
- o ½ Tsp. salt
- o ½ Tsp. ground pepper
- o 1 Cup Asiago cheese, finely shredded

1. Boil pasta in a large pot for 10 minutes. Drain away water and return pasta to pot.

2. While pasta is boiling, use a large skillet to heat the oil on medium. Add in mushrooms and sprouts. Cook for 10 minutes, stirring occasionally. Add garlic and continue cooking for 1 additional minute. Add in sherry, making sure to

scrap up the brown bits. Bring it to a boil until the sherry evaporates. It takes about 10 seconds.

3. Whisk milk and flour on a bowl to the side. Then add mixture to skillet, sprinkling in salt and pepper. Cook approximately 2 minutes, or until the sauce thickens. Mix in Asiago until it fully melts.

4. Add sauce to pasta.

Macros (per serving)

Calories: 384

Fat: 10g.

Carbs: 56g.

Protein: 18g

Curried Cauliflower Steaks with Red Rice

Servings: 4

- o   2 heads of cauliflower

- o   1 Cup red or brown rice

- o   1/3 Cup extra-virgin olive oil

- o   1 Tbsp. lemon juice

- o   2 Tsp. curry powder

- o   ½ Tsp. kosher salt

- o   2 Tbsp. fresh cilantro, chopped

1. Preheat oven to 450 degrees. Line a large baking sheet with tin foil.

2. Follow directions to prepare rice.

3. Whisk together oil, curry powder, and salt in a bowl.

4. Prepare cauliflower, making sure to keep stems intact. Place stem-side down on a cutting board and cut into thick slices to create "steaks." Get 4 steaks. Then slice the remaining cauliflower into smaller slices to get 4 cups.

5. Place steaks and florets onto a baking sheet. Brush both sides of the steaks with the curry mixture.

6. Place steaks in oven, turning after 15 minutes. Finish baking until steaks are tender and brown.

7. Divide rice evenly onto 4 plates and top each plate with a cauliflower steak. Sprinkle with cilantro.

Note: You can refrigerate cauliflower for up to 3 days so you can prepare it ahead of time if needed.

Macros (per serving)

Calories: 410

Fat: 21g.

Carbs: 49g.

Protein: 10g

Egg with Salsa and Toast

Servings: 1

- ○ 1 egg, either boiled or cooked in ¼ tsp. Olive Oil

- ○ 2 Tbsp. Salsa

- ○ 1 Slice of toasted bread, whole wheat

- ○ Small pinch of salt and pepper (optional)

1. Spread egg, salsa, and salt/pepper on top of toast.

Macros (per serving)

Calories: 180

Fat: 10g.

Carbs: 13g.

Protein: 10g

Fig and Honey Yogurt

Servings: 1

- o 2/3 Cup Greek yogurt, nonfat and plain

- o 5 Chopped figs, dry

- o 2 Tsp. chia seeds

- o 1 ½ Tsp. honey

1. Top yogurt with chia seeds, figs, and honey.

Macros (per serving)

Calories: 208

Fat: 3g.

Carbs: 39g.

Protein: 9g

Gazpacho with Chickpeas

Servings: 6

- o 15 Oz. can of chickpeas, drained and rinsed thoroughly

- o 6 Cups vegetable juice, unsalted with no added sugar

- o 1 Cup cherry tomatoes cut in quarters

- o ¼ Red onion, chopped

- o ½ Cup seeded, chopped cucumber

- o ¼ Cup fresh cilantro, chopped

- o ¼ Tsp. hot pepper sauce

- o 1 Minced garlic clove

- o ¼ Cup lime juice

- o 6 Lime wedges

1. Mix together tomatoes, cucumber, chickpeas, vegetable juice, hot pepper sauce, lime juice, garlic, onion, and cilantro in a bowl.

2. Cover bowl and store in the fridge for one hour.

3. Serve the soup cold in small bowls with one lime wedge.

This dish can be stored for several days so you can enjoy several meals from it. It's a great, easy dish for those super busy weeks.

Macros (per serving)

Calories: 125

Fat: 1g.

Carbs: 24g.

Protein: 7g

Green Salad with Pita Bread and Hummus

Servings: 1

- o   2 Cups mixed greens

- o   ¼ Carrot, grated

- o   ½ Cup cucumber, sliced

- o   2 Tbsp. Vinaigrette

- o   ½ Large pita, whole-wheat

- o   ¼ Cup hummus

1. Spread greens onto a plate and top with cucumber, carrot, and vinaigrette. Serve with pita bread and hummus.

Macros (per serving)

Calories: 374

Fat: 14g.

Carbs: 53g.

Protein: 14g

Grilled Asian Salmon

Servings: 1

- 2 Salmon fillets, 4 Oz. each

- ½ Tbsp. sesame oil

- 1 Tbsp. low-sodium soy sauce

- 1 Tbsp. minced ginger

- ½ Tbsp. rice wine vinegar

1. Using a shallow glass dish, mix together sesame oil, soy sauce, ginger, and vinegar.

2. Add salmon to mix. Thoroughly coat each side. Then place in the refrigerator for 1 hour, turning every 15 minutes.

3. Oil grill lightly and preheat to medium-high. Place salmon onto the grill and cook for 5 minutes on each side. You will know the fish is fully cooked when you can insert a knife, turn and see that the pink flesh has become opaque.

Note: Serve while warm. You can reheat in microwave and serve that same day. Do not store longer than 12 hours.

Macros (per serving)

Calories: 374

Fat: 14g.

Carbs: 53g.

Protein: 14g

Hard-Boiled Egg, Bacon, and Juice

Servings: 1

o   1-6 Eggs

o   2 Slices Canadian Bacon

o   6 Oz. low sodium tomato juice (no added sugar)

1. Hard boil eggs. I recommend you boil at least 6 eggs, peel, and then store them in a storage container in the fridge so you have access to them in the coming week.

2. Cook bacon in a skillet using no added fats. Serve with eggs and tomato juice.

Macros (per serving)

Calories: 160

Fat: 9g.

Carbs: 2g.

Protein: 18g

Lemon-Garlic Shrimp over Orzo with Zucchini

Servings: 4

o 1 ½ Lbs. large shrimp in shells, either fresh or frozen

o 2 Lemons

o ¾ Cup orzo pasta, dried

o 2 Tbsp. olive oil

o 1 Tbsp. butter, unsalted

o 3 Cloves minced garlic

o 1/8 Tsp. red pepper, crushed

o 2 Cups zucchini, sliced

o ¼ Cup shallots, thinly sliced

o ¼ Tsp. black pepper

o 2 Tbsp. water

o 1 Tsp. fresh rosemary, snipped

o 2 Tbsp. fresh dill weed, snipped

1. Peel shrimp. You can leave tails intact if you want. Thoroughly rinse shrimp and use a paper towel to pat them dry.

2. Remove zest from 1 lemon using a vegetable peeler, cutting into thin slivers. Squeeze ¼ cup of juice from lemons. You should have half a lemon left. Place it to the side.

3. Prepare orzo following the instructions on the package. Leave out any salt and fat.

4. Heat up oil and butter in a nonstick skillet on medium-high. Add in shrimp, 2 cloves of garlic, ¼ tsp. salt, and crushed red pepper.

5. Cook shrimp for approximately 2 minutes or until they are opaque. Mix in lemon juice.

6. Remove from heat and cover so that it stays warm.

7. Heat remaining oil in the skillet. Add zucchini, shallots, pepper, and the remaining garlic clove and ¼ tsp. salt. Cook for 3 minutes until the zucchini is light brown.

8. Add in rosemary, water, and the rest of the lemon juice. Stir so that you scrap up the crusty bits. Mix in the cooked orzo.

9. Stir in shrimp mix and sprinkle with dill and slivers of lemon. Finally, squeeze the juice from the remaining half lemon over the mixture.

Macros (per serving)

Calories: 355

Fat: 11g.

Carbs: 30g.

Protein: 35g

Lemon-Herb Salmon with Caponata and Farro

Servings: 4

- o 2 cups water
- o 1 ¼ lbs. Wild salmon cut into 4 equal-sized portions
- o ⅔ cup farro
- o 1 Eggplant (medium), cut into one-inch cubes
- o 1 Bell pepper (Red), cut into one-inch pieces
- o 1 Summer squash, cut into one-inch pieces
- o 1 Small onion, cut into one-inch pieces
- o 1 ½ Cup cherry tomato
- o 3 Tbsp. extra-virgin olive oil
- o ¾ Tsp. salt
- o ½ Tsp. pepper, ground
- o 2 Tbsp. capers, chopped
- o 1 Tbsp. red-wine vinegar
- o 2 Tsp. honey
- o 1 Tsp. lemon zest
- o ½ Tsp. Italian seasoning
- o Lemon wedges

1. Racks in oven should be positioned in the upper and lower thirds. Preheat oven to 450 Degrees.

2. Line 2 baking sheets with tin foil and coat foil with cooking spray.

3. Farro and water should be brought to a boil. Then reduce the heat to low and simmer for approximately 30 minutes or until tender. Drain.

4. Mix eggplant, bell pepper, squash, onion and tomatoes with oil, ½ teaspoon salt and ¼ teaspoon pepper in a large bowl. Then divide it amongst the baking sheets that you have already prepared.

5. Place vegetables on the upper and lower racks of the oven for approximately 25 minutes. You will need to stir about halfway through baking. Once they are brown and tender, mix them with capers, vinegar, and honey.

6. Sprinkle lemon zest onto salmon, Italian seasoning, and ¼ Tsp. of salt and pepper. Place them onto one of the baking sheets. Bake on lower rack for 6-12 minutes or until it's cooked thoroughly.

7. Serve Salmon with faro, vegetable caponata, and lemon wedges.

<u>Macros (per serving)</u>

Calories: 450

Fat: 17g.

Carbs: 41g.

Protein: 35g

Mediterranean Chicken with Orzo Salad

Servings: 4

- o   2 skinless, boneless chicken breasts cut into halves
- o   3 Tbsp. extra-virgin olive oil
- o   1 Tsp. lemon zest
- o   ½ Tsp. salt
- o   ½ Tsp. pepper
- o   ¾ Cup whole-wheat orzo
- o   2 Cups baby spinach, thinly sliced
- o   1 Cup cucumber, chopped
- o   1 Cup tomato, chopped
- o   ¼ Cup red onion, chopped
- o   ¼ Cup feta cheese, crumbled
- o   2 Tbsp. Kalamata onions, chopped
- o   2 Tbsp. lemon juice
- o   1 clove garlic, grated
- o   2 Tsp. fresh oregano, chopped

1. Preheat over at 425 degrees

2. Brush 1 tbsp. olive oil over chicken and then sprinkle with lemon zest and ¼ tsp. salt and pepper. Place chicken into a baking dish.

3. Bake 30 minutes or until thermometer registers at 165 degrees into the chicken.

4. While chicken is baking in the oven, bring a saucepan of water to a boil. Add orzo and then cook for approximately 8 minutes. Add spinach and cook for 1 additional minute. Drain and then rinse with cold water.

5. Transfer spinach and orzo to a large bowl. Add cucumber, tomato, onion, feta, and olives. Mix together.

6. In a small bowl, whisk remaining olive oil, lemon juice oregano, salt, and pepper. Then mix just 1 tbsp. of the dressing mix into the orzo mixture. Drizzle remaining 1 tbsp. over chicken and serve with the salad.

Macros (per serving)

Calories: 400

Fat: 7g.

Carbs: 28g.

Protein: 32g

Mediterranean-Style Chicken Kabobs

Servings: 10

- 1.5 Lbs. skinless, boneless chicken thighs cut into pieces (approximately 40)

- 1 Red bell pepper, cut into pieces

- 2 Tbsp. extra-virgin olive oil

- 1 Minced garlic clove

- 1 Tsp. oregano, dried

- ½ Tsp. dried basil

- ¾ Tsp. salt

- ¼ Tsp. black pepper, ground

- 1 Lemon cut into wedges

1. Mix chicken, bell peppers, olive oil, garlic, oregano, and basil into a large bowl. Place in the fridge for 30 minutes.

2. Preheat broiler. While waiting, lightly spread oil on a broiler pan.

3. Skewer 5 pieces of chicken, 4 bell peppers, alternatively onto skewers. Create as many skewers as possible. Sprinkle with salt and pepper.

4. Place skewers onto broiling pan and place in broiler. They should be approximately 5 inches from the heat source.

Cook for 8-10 minutes, turning every 2 minutes until chicken is fully cooked.

5. Serve with lemon wedges.

Macros (per serving)

Calories: 228

Fat: 17g.

Carbs: 6g.

Protein: 14g

Mini-Egg Beaters Southwestern Style Omelet

Servings: 1

- o   15-30 Oz. box Egg Beaters Southwestern Style

- o   1 Tbsp. extra virgin olive oil

1. Spread oil over skillet.

2. Add ½ Cup of Egg Beaters Southwestern Style mix. Cook on medium until fully cooked.

Macros (per serving)

Calories: 500

Fat: 8g.

Carbs: 0g.

Protein: 20g

Peanut-Butter Cinnamon Toast

Servings: 1

- o 1 Slice toasted bread, whole-wheat

- o 1 Tbsp. peanut butter

- o 1 banana

- o Cinnamon (to taste)

1. Spread peanut butter onto toast. Top it with banana slices. Then sprinkle with cinnamon to taste.

Macros (per serving)

Calories: 266

Fat: 9g.

Carbs: 38g.

Protein: 8g

Quinoa Meatless Balls

Servings: 12

- o   2 ½ Cup quinoa, cooked
- o   4 Eggs
- o   ½ Tsp. salt
- o   1/3 Cup chives
- o   1 Onion
- o   1/3 Cup parmesan cheese, grated
- o   3 Cloves garlic
- o   1 ¾ Cup bread crumbs, whole grain
- o   1 Tbsp. extra virgin olive oil

1. Combine ingredients in a large bowl. Mix thoroughly.

2. Using your hands, create meatballs from the mixture.

3. Coat a skillet with olive oil.

4. Cook meatballs in the skillet for approximately 10 minutes, until brown.

Macros (per serving)

Calories: 291

Fat: 10g.

Carbs: 139g.

Protein: 13g

Salmon Pita Sandwich

Servings: 1

- 2 Tbsp. yogurt, plain and nonfat

- 3 ounces flaked, canned sockeye salmon

- Half of a 6-inch whole-wheat pita bread

- ½ Cup watercress

- 2 Tsp. chopped, fresh dill

- 2 Tsp. lemon juice

- ½ Tsp. horseradish

1. Mix yogurt, lemon juice, and horseradish in a small bowl. Stir in salmon.

2. Stuff pita bread with salmon mixture and watercress. The ratio should be 50/50.

Macros (per serving)

Calories: 239

Fat: 7g.

Carbs: 19g.

Protein: 25g

Stuffed Sweet Potato with Hummus Dressing

Servings: 1

- o 1 Sweet potato, scrubbed

- o ¾ Cup kale, chopped

- o 1 Cup canned black beans, rinsed

- o ¼ Cup hummus

- o 2 Tbsp. water

1. Poke small holes into the sweet potato using a fork. Microwave on high until it's fully cooked.

2. Wash kale and allow a small amount of water to cling to leaves. Place into a saucepan, cover, and cook on medium. Stir 2 times before adding beans and add 1 tbsp. water if pot is dry. Cook until mixture is steaming hot.

3. Cut open the sweet potato and top with the kale mixture. Combine hummus and 2 tbsp. water in a separate dish. Add additional water if needed.

4. Drizzle hummus dressing over sweet potatoes.

Macros (per serving)

Calories: 472

Fat: 7g.

Carbs: 85g.

Protein: 21g

Tuna Salad Sandwich

Servings: 2 (read note)

- o 1 Can white tuna, unsalted and packed in water

- o ¼ Cup celery, diced

- o ½ Tsp. lemon juice

- o ¼ Cup low-calorie mayonnaise

- o 2 Slices bread, whole-wheat

1. Fluff tuna with a fork in a small bowl and then add the rest of the ingredients. Mix thoroughly.

2. Spread the mixture evenly over one slice of bread so that you create two sandwiches.

Note: You will have half of the mixture left over. You can make another sandwich with it later. It can be stored in the refrigerator for up to one day.

Macros (per serving)

Calories: 240

Fat: 3g.

Carbs: 24g.

Protein: 19g

Turkey and Pear Pita Melt

Servings: 1

- ½ Large pita, whole-wheat

- 1 Pear cut into slices

- 3 ½ Oz. deli turkey (low sodium if possible)

- 1 Tbsp. cheddar cheese, shredded

- 1 Cup mixed greens

1. Stuff pita with pear slices, cheese, and turkey.

2. Place in a toaster over until the cheese melts.

3. Add greens just before eating.

Note: You can eat the rest of the pear slices with the melt.

Macros (per serving)

Calories: 490

Fat: 27g.

Carbs: 29g.

Protein: 33g

Turkey Wrap

Servings: 6

- o 12 Oz. low-sodium sliced deli turkey

- o ¼ Cup mashed avocado

- o ¼ Cup salsa

- o 2 Tortillas, whole-wheat

- o 1 Cup green cabbage, shredded

- o ½ Cup carrots, thinly slices

- o ½ Cup tomatoes, sliced

1. Mix avocado and salsa thoroughly and spread it evenly across both tortillas.

2. Distribute the remainder of ingredients evenly across the center of both tortillas.

3. Fold tortillas and cut them in half. Store remainder in plastic bag so you can enjoy them later.

Macros (per serving)

Calories: 347

Fat: 21g.

Carbs: 34g.

Protein: 20g

Veggie-Hummus Sandwich

Servings: 1

- 2 Slices of bread, whole-grain

- ¼ Avocado, mashed

- 3 Tbsp. Hummus

- ½ Cup salad greens

- ¼ Medium bell pepper, red and sliced

- ¼ Cup sliced cucumber

- ¼ Cup shredded carrot

1. Spread hummus on one side of bread and avocado on the other side.

2. Fill the sandwich with the remainder of ingredients.

3. Slice in half.

Note: You can make this 4 hours ahead of time if you store it in the refrigerator.

Macros (per serving)

Calories: 325

Fat: 14g.

Carbs: 40g.

Protein: 13g

White Bean and Avocado Toast

Servings: 1

- o 1 Slice of toast, whole-wheat

- o ½ Avocado, mashed

- o ¼ Cap white beans, mashed and rinsed

- o Salt to taste

- o Pepper to taste

- o Crushed red pepper (optional)

1. Top toast with avocado and white beans. Season with salt, pepper, and red pepper.

Macros (per serving)

Calories: 270

Fat: 16g.

Carbs: 29g.

Protein: 9g

White Bean and Avocado Salad

Servings: 1

- 2 Cups salad greens, mixed and fresh

- ¾ Cup fresh vegetables chopped, your choice.

- 1/3 Cup canned white beans

- One-Half of an avocado, diced

- 2 Tbsp. All-Purpose Vinaigrette

1. Toss everything together in a bowl to create your delicious salad.

Macros (per serving)

Calories: 320

Fat: 18g.

Carbs: 16g.

Protein: 14g

Yogurt with Nuts and Raspberries

Servings: 1

o   1 Cup Green yogurt, plain and nonfat

o   ½ Cup raspberries

o   5 Walnuts, chopped

o   1 Tsp. honey

1. Place raspberries, honey, and walnuts on top of yogurt.

Macros (per serving)

Calories: 250

Fat: 4.5g.

Carbs: 35g.

Protein: 19g

Get an Audio Book for FREE!

Don't have an Audible account?

Sign up and get "The Everyday DASH Diet Guide" audio book for FREE!

http://bit.ly/kelso-dash-diet

One Last Thing… Did You Enjoy the Book?

If so, then let me know by leaving a review on Amazon! Reviews are the lifeblood of independent authors. I would appreciate even a few words from you!

If you did not like the book, then please tell me! Email me at lizard.publishing@gmail.com and let me know what you didn't like. Perhaps I can change it. In today's world, a book doesn't have to be stagnant. It should be improved with time and feedback from readers like you. You can impact this book, and I welcome your feedback. Help me make this book better for everyone!